D1129612

MAXIMAL ECONOMIC GROWTH

A Geometric Approach to Von Neumann's Growth Theory and the Turnpike Theorem

MAXIMAL ECONOMIC GROWTH

A Geometric Approach to Von Neumann's Growth Theory and the Turnpike Theorem

JAROSLAV VANEK

Cornell University Press • ITHACA, NEW YORK

First published 1968

Library of Congress Catalog Card Number: 68-28807

PRINTED IN THE UNITED STATES OF AMERICA
BY THE SCIENCE PRESS, INC.
BOUND BY VAIL-BALLOU PRESS, INC.

To my students

Preface

As is so often the case, the present study has evolved from an initial effort which was considerably less ambitious. Faced with difficulties virtually insurmountable to many of my students and to myself in trying to decipher the literature on Von Neumann's theory of growth and the turnpike theorem, I originally intended to write a set of intelligible notes for my graduate course in economic theory. The task turned out to be more absorbing than I had expected, and in the end the course was over before I had any material to show to my students. With a feeling that I owed them something and realizing that in substance and methodology there was in my approach a good deal that was new, I decided to polish my notes once they were completed and have them published. Thereby I am able not only to do away with my debt but also, I hope, to assist other students of economic theory, on both sides of the desk, who may have experienced similar difficulties in coping with a highly technical literature.

JAROSLAV VANEK

Ithaca, New York
January 1968

Contents

Figures

MAXIMAL ECONOMIC GROWTH

A Geometric Approach to Von Neumann's Growth Theory and the Turnpike Theorem

I. Introduction

Originating in the works of Ramsey and Von Neumann and revitalized in more recent years by writings such as Dorfman, Samuelson, and Solow's study in linear programing, the subject of growth efficiency has come to occupy a prominent place on the frontier of economic theory.[1] Unfortunately, a comparatively large segment of our profession, including the present writer, and including even a number of economists normally recognized as theorists, find it difficult and sometimes impossible to follow the various mathematical arguments, derivations, and proofs of this part of economic theory.

One of the purposes of this study is to translate an important segment of the theory of efficient growth—specifically, Von Neumann's growth model with its turnpike extensions—into simple, nonmathematical language. Thus I hope to make the model accessible to many of my fellow nonmathematical economists and to students who have not, or have not yet, mastered advanced mathematical methods. In fact, the only technical prerequisite for understanding the subsequent chapters is a

[1] F. Ramsey, "A Mathematical Theory of Saving," *Economic Journal*, XXXVIII (1928), 543–559; J. Von Neumann, "A Model of General Economic Equilibrium," *Review of Economic Studies,* XIII (1945–1946), 1–9; R. Dorfman, P. A. Samuelson, and R. M. Solow, *Linear Programming and Economic Analysis* (New York, 1958).

familiarity with the production box-diagram and the various geometric relationships the diagram involves.[2] The only cost we have to pay for this simplicity in most of the present analysis is the use of a single-product technology instead of the joint-product technologies customarily encountered in works dealing with the problem. But this method should not be a serious hindrance, at least to an economist, especially because the use of joint products does not modify the results too significantly. Moreover, in the concluding chapter we will relax the no-joint-product assumption and show the corresponding key results.

For the reader entirely unfamiliar with the subject on which we are about to enter, it may be useful to explain the problem in plain words. The world of the Von Neumann and turnpike theories is a highly abstract one, where, period after period, capital goods are produced from identical goods used as inputs in the preceding period according to some prescribed technological relationship. Man can enter the process, if at all, only as a material itself reproduced through inputs of men and goods. In such a world the rate and direction (in terms of structural composition) of development will depend on how resources are allocated in each of the productive periods; the principal aim of the Von Neumann and turnpike theories is to identify and study the nature of allocations which are efficient, that is, which maximize the rate of growth of the economy.

I realize that as a general rule translations from mathematical into nonmathematical English have not yet ac-

[2]One source explaining the geometry of the box diagram is chap. 12 of my *International Trade* (Homewood, Ill., 1962).

quired professional respectability in our field.[3] And thus, if I have dared submit this study for publication, it was because I believe that it can also have other significance. In particular, it is hoped that even those on the frontier of economic theory—or perhaps of applied mathematics—will find useful some of the subsequent analysis, method, and findings.

The turnpike theorem is stated here with a somewhat greater generality than usual—with reference to both oscillatory and "smooth" trajectories—and is proved without the customary reference to an (inefficient) *comparison path* (involved, for example, in the Radner proof).[4] What is more important, the proof here offered, especially its variant pertaining to fixed-coefficient technologies, can be explained without difficulty to first-year undergraduate students of economics. The method of showing and proving the turnpike theorem chosen here lends itself, moreover, to an easy evaluation of the orders of magnitude (or, more descriptively, orders of smallness) of some of the key parameters involved in the statement of the turnpike theorem. For example, in a situation of long-range growth with fixed coefficients over one hundred periods, the minimum angular distance between the Von Neumann path and any actual efficient path hardly will exceed 10^{-40} of a degree, if we assume that the range of the factor proportions of the technologies involved is no more than 100 per cent (a limiting case

[3] J. R. Hicks, *Value and Capital* (Oxford, 1965), is one significant exception.

[4] R. Radner, "Paths of Economic Growth That Are Optimal with Regard Only to Final States: A Turnpike Theorem," *Review of Economic Studies*, XXVIII (1961), 98–104.

would be where the proportions in one industry were 1 to 1 and in the other 2 to 1). It is interesting to note that the minimum angular distance in the case just referred to must arise in the second production period. The simplicity of analytical tools employed makes it possible in a number of instances to gain insights—even if such insights are not always embodied in rigorously stated and fully proved theorems—which otherwise would be hard to obtain. For example, some basic "rules of conduct" for efficient paths can easily be established: one such rule is that *smooth* (nonoscillatory) efficient paths intersecting the Von Neumann path must be single-valued with respect to a ray through the origin, and other *smooth* paths can at most be double-valued. Another instance of a fruitful application of the nonmathematical tools is found in the extension of Von Neumann's analysis and its turnpike generalizations to the case of nonzero consumption. Alternatively, it is not too difficult to examine, along similar lines, such Von Neumann growth situations as those involving identical technologies, technological change, and large numbers of inputs and outputs.

But before we get to these refinements, we have first to develop systematically the conventional theory, starting with what is most basic and rudimentary—the definition of the growth model. As we have mentioned already, we begin with a world involving single-product technologies. Moreover, the hard core of our analysis is cast within the neoclassical framework of smooth technologies and constant returns to scale. Only in some of the later chapters do we reconsider a number of the key results on the assumption of fixed-coefficient (or Leontief-type) technologies.

Finally it ought to be pointed out that in its explanatory or popularizing role the present study is not alone. There are at least two other works, one by Koopmans, the other by Hicks, that fulfill basically the same function.[5] With respect to those two works, the position of this monograph can be thought of as "somewhere in between" in the sense that it tries to attain the same degree of rigor as does Koopmans' while using an approach no more difficult than that of Hicks's more popular exposition.

[5] T. C. Koopmans, "Economic Growth at a Maximal Rate," *Quarterly Journal of Economics*, LXXVIII (1964), 355–394; Hicks, *Capital and Growth* (Oxford, 1965).

II. The growth model defined

The characteristics of the idealized dynamic world which we examine in the subsequent ten chapters are as follows: In each period t two products, $\bar{x}_t$ and $\bar{y}_t$, are produced in separate processes from physically identical inputs, x_{t-1} and y_{t-1}, in the preceding period, $t-1$. A bar on top of a variable is used to indicate a supply, or output, while variables without bars represent inputs. The two processes, given by

$$\bar{x}_t = f_1(x^x_{t-1}, y^x_{t-1}) \tag{1}$$

and

$$\bar{y}_t = f_2(x^y_{t-1}, y^y_{t-1}) \tag{2}$$

are subject to constant returns to scale[6] and are perfectly invariant over time; the isoquants are smooth and convex toward the origin; on the limit, at their extremities, they can be parallel to, or even coincide with, the axes. The outputs in each period are used in full as inputs in that period:

$$\bar{x}_t = x^x_t + x^y_t \tag{3}$$

and

$$\bar{y}_t = y^x_t + y^y_t \tag{4}$$

[6]More rigorously, by this we mean production functions satisfying, for any ϕ, $\phi\bar{x} = f_1(\phi x^x_{t-1}, \phi y^x_{t-1})$ and $\phi\bar{y}_t = f_2(\phi x^y_{t-1}, \phi y^y_{t-1})$.

In each period the static allocation of productive resources between the two sectors is Pareto-optimal; that is, the marginal rates of substitution in the two industries are equal. More descriptively, in the production box-diagram (defined for each period) we are always on the contract curve.

Furthermore—again for the subsequent ten chapters—we make the assumption of a uniform factor-intensity relationship between the two production functions.[7] This assumption leaves us with three cases: that where product $\overline{y}$ is always relatively y-intensive and $\overline{x}$ is x-intensive; that where $\overline{y}$ is always x-intensive and $\overline{x}$ y-intensive; and that where the two production functions have identical factor proportions for identical factor prices. For reasons which will become more apparent later, we will refer hereafter to the first case as the S-case and to the second as the Z-case.[8]

The hypothetical economy is endowed with an initial bundle of inputs $A_0 = (x_0, y_0)$. It then proceeds, in subsequent periods 1, 2, 3, . . . , to transform the initial endowment A_0 into subsequent output and input points through the process just described and summarized in relations (1) through (4), thus generating a sequence of points in the x-y plane $A_0, A_1, \ldots, A_n$—where n is the total number of periods considered. This sequence we

[7]The production function of $\overline{x}$ is said to be uniformly (input) x-intensive relative to the production function of y, provided that for any prescribed marginal rate of substitution (between inputs) x is produced with a higher x/y ratio than y. It should also be noted that the condition has no simple equivalent statement in terms of elasticities of substitution of the technologies x and y.

[8]The letter S stands for "smooth" and Z for "zigzag," and the respective qualifications refer to the nature of the corresponding growth path.

call a *growth path* and denote it by A. The general purpose of this work is an extensive study, as comprehensive as possible, of the nature and properties of the various conceivable paths.

III. Intertemporally efficient and inefficient paths

Let us take a somewhat closer look at the growth process defined in Chapter II; in so doing, we shall establish an important distinction between *intertemporally inefficient* and *efficient* paths. Figure 1 summarizes all the data of the growth situation. The endowment point A_0 tells us how much of x and y the economy has initially at its disposal. The isoquants *aa* and *bb*—corresponding to outputs $\bar{x} = a$ and $\bar{y} = b$—define the two single-product and linear-homogeneous production functions; the former isoquant reflects inputs measured from the origin $0(x)$, while the latter reflects inputs measured from point A_1. It will be noted that the growth situation thus defined is of the *S*-variety, because $\bar{x}$ is x-intensive and $\bar{y}$ is y-intensive. Whatever is shown in this chapter pertains equally to the *Z*-variety, however, as the reader may verify. The special situation of identical or similar technologies will be treated in Chapter XI.

The initial endowment A_0 generates in period 1 (through the customary production box construction) a transformation locus (production possibility, or opportunity-cost curve) T_1, which is maximal in the sense that collections of products $\bar{x}$ and $\bar{y}$ northeast of T_1 cannot be attained in that period. Only points on that locus interest us in period 1, because with given inputs it would be irrational to produce less than the feasible maximum. Any of the points on T_1 can be chosen in period 1 as an input point to generate output in period 2. Suppose that A_1 is such a point. As shown in Figure 1, it defines a production box, and the contract curve (efficiency locus) running between the origin $0(x)$ and A_1 shows all the statically efficient allocations of inputs (given by A_1) between the two industries. The outputs corresponding to all points on the contract curve are represented by the locus t_2.

If we consider all points on T_1 such as A_1, construct loci such as t_2 for each of them, and then draw the en-

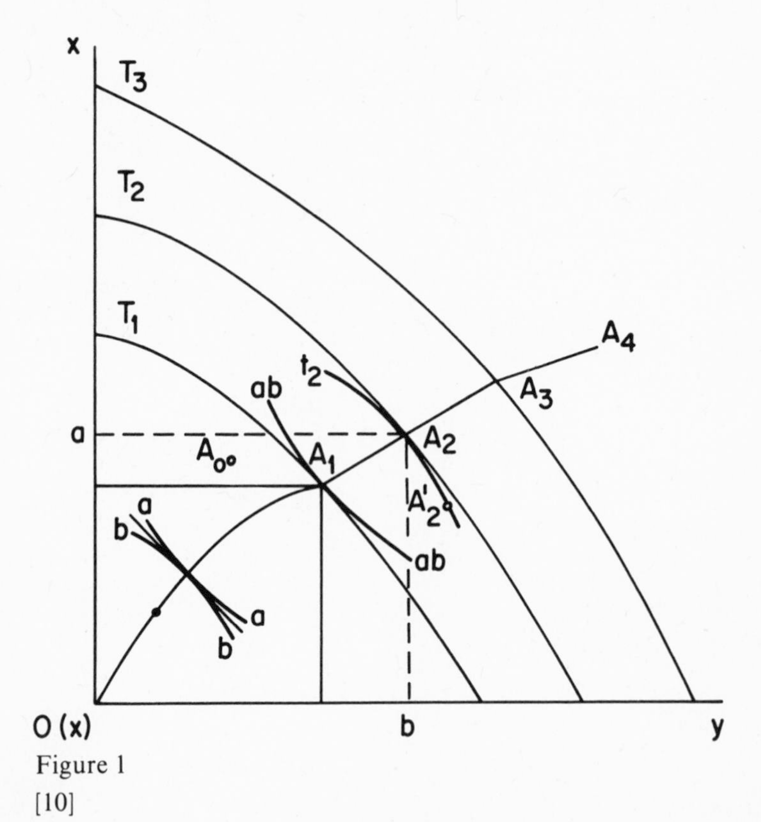

Figure 1

velope of these loci, we will find the contour T_2, which is the locus of maximum levels of output of $\bar{x}$ and $\bar{y}$ attainable in period 2, given the prescribed technologies and given the initial endowment point A_0. That it is *attainable* is apparent from the fact that all points on T_1 are attainable and that each point on T_2 is also a point on a production possibility such as t_2. That it is a locus of *maximum* outputs follows from the facts that T_1 is maximum (given A_0) and that T_2 is an envelope of statically Pareto-optimal loci (such as t_2).

A locus of maximum attainable outputs in period 3, T_3, can then be obtained from T_2 in the same way as T_2 was obtained from T_1, and so forth for $T_4, T_5, \ldots, T_n$. Each such locus then represents a collection of "maximal" points attainable from A_0 after 2, 3, 4, 5, ..., and n periods.

Let us now consider a single path leading from lower to higher transformation loci T_i. Suppose that the path we want to consider passes through A_1 in the diagram, so that we already have the first stage of the path, A_0A_1. That stage is efficient because A_1 is on T_1. As shown in the diagram, the second stage leads to A_2, the point where t_2 is tangential to the envelope T_2. This must be so because from A_1 only points on t_2 can be attained, and, at the same time, A_2 must be on T_2. The coordinates of A_2, outputs $\bar{x} = a$ and $\bar{y} = b$, are produced from resources indicated by A_1 through an allocation of those resources given by the point of tangency between isoquants *aa* and *bb*. The important characteristic of that resource allocation is that the marginal rates of substitution in both industries are equal to the marginal rate of transformation at A_1.

As we will show presently, this equality becomes the

important condition of intertemporal efficiency, guaranteeing that the expansion path leads from one optimal locus T_i to another. There is also any number of intertemporally inefficient paths starting from A_1 in Figure 1 and leading to any other point on t_2 except A_2. The segment of the efficient path A_1A_2, it also will be shown, is unique in the sense that for a given point on T_1 (such as A_1) there can be only one efficient point on T_2 (such as A_2); however, there will be many points on T_1 (and similarly on any higher T_i) which will not have a corresponding efficient point on T_2 (or on T_{i+1}).

To show the condition of intertemporal efficiency, consider in Figure 1 the locus *ab-ab* passing through A_1 and tangential to T_1. Its property—perfectly analogous to that of the so-called Scitovsky indifference curve[9]—is that its points represent the minimum amounts of x and y necessary to produce outputs of $\bar{x} = a$ and $\bar{y} = b$ (that is, the coordinates of A_2). It is obtained by sliding back to back the isoquants *aa* and *bb*, tracing a contour by means of the northeast corner of the corresponding box diagram and holding the origin $0(x)$ fixed. Given such a construction, the slope of *ab-ab* at A_1 must equal the common slope of *bb* and *aa* (marginal rates of substitution in the two industries) as well as the slope of T_1 (the marginal rate of transformation at A_1).

Suppose that any Pareto-optimal allocation of productive resources other than that corresponding to the isoquants *aa* and *bb* were selected on the contract curve $0(x)A_1$; there would again be a locus of points, analogous to *ab-ab*, indicating the minimum amounts of x and y necessary to produce the new composition of outputs

[9] For example, see T. Scitovsky, "A Reconsideration of the Theory of Tariffs," *Review of Economic Studies*, (1942).

(say, the composition indicated by A_2', necessarily on t_2). Such a new locus could not be tangential to T_1 at A_1, however; rather, because of the uniformly changing common marginal rates of substitution as we move along the contract curve from $0(x)$ to A_1 in Figure 1, it would intersect T_1. But this intersection would necessarily imply that the point A_2' is producible with less resources than those allowable by T_1 for period 1 and, consequently, that more of both $\bar{x}$ and $\bar{y}$ could have been produced than is indicated by A_2'. Of course, we know this already, because t_2 is below T_2 at that point. What we did not know, and what we have just shown, is that in order to get the intertemporally efficient solution—a point such as A_2 on T_2—the slopes of *ab-ab* and T_1 at A_1 must be the same. Moreover, from the fact that for two different homogeneous production functions the same marginal rate of substitution cannot be encountered along a contract curve more than once, it follows that *ab-ab* and, thus, the efficient point A_2 on T_2 are unique.

At this stage of the argument one point must be made which will be of considerable importance in our subsequent analysis: There will be many points on T_1 where the marginal rate of transformation will not be equaled by any set of marginal rates of substitution along the corresponding contract curve. Such points on T_1—which, as will be shown later, occur at its extremities—will have no efficient correspondence on T_2, and similarly for points on any pair of loci T_i and T_{i+1}.

We are now in a position to define intertemporally efficient expansion paths as paths which fulfill in each period the intertemporal efficiency condition just explained (of course, besides the static Pareto-optimality always claimed). In other words, we are defining as intertemporally efficient all paths leading from points on the efficient frontiers (T_1) to other such frontiers. All other paths are intertemporally inefficient. With one important exception (see Chapter IV), we will concern ourselves in this study with paths which are intertemporally efficient. For simplicity's sake we shall henceforth drop the qualification "intertemporally."

It follows from what has been shown in this chapter that besides the initial endowment and relations (1) through (4) already postulated, an efficient path A is entirely determined once a point on T_1, such as A_1, is selected. Through the property of uniqueness of correspondence between consecutive efficient points (such as A_1 and A_2 or A_2 and A_3 in Figure 1) explained above, all subsequent points of the path—finite or infinite in number—are determined. It also follows that once A_1, and hence the marginal rate of transformation at A_1, is given, the marginal rates of transformation at all consecutive points $A_i (i = 2, 3, 4, \ldots)$ are also known. The variation of the marginal rates associated with a movement along an efficient path will be discussed in the following chapter. First, however, we must make a few observations concerning the relationship between market conditions and intertemporal efficiency.

In defining and explaining intertemporal efficiency we have thus far used purely technical criteria; in a given period the marginal rates of substitution in production (also equal to the slope of the corresponding Scitovsky isoquant) must equal the marginal rate of transformation along the efficient frontier T_i of that period, at the point of actual output and resource utilization. For the planning board of a fully planned economy whose sole concern it would be never to depart from an efficient frontier, the criteria would be perfectly adequate. It must also be noted, however, using an analogy with an argument well known from static general equilibrium analysis, that the "invisible hand" inherent in perfectly competitive markets would lead precisely to the conditions of intertemporal efficiency. Specifically, on the assumption of perfect competition, relative product prices would be equal to both the marginal rate of transformation between outputs of a given period and the marginal rates of substitution of inputs in the same period; and thus the two different marginal rates would be equal to each other.

Throughout this study we make the assumption of a perfectly competitive world. Consequently, we can speak of equilibrium marginal conditions interchangeably in terms of relative prices and in terms of marginal rates, the two alternatives being always equivalent.

IV. Price variations associated with efficient paths

Given the assumptions we have made—in particular, linear homogeneity of production functions and perfect competition—a set of input prices uniquely determines prices of outputs. Coupled with the requirement of intertemporal efficiency shown in the preceding chapter, this correspondence between input and output prices (marginal rates) makes it easy to study the variation of relative prices of x and y, $R(= p_y/p_x)$, as we proceed from A_0 along an efficient path A.

Suppose that the linear-homogeneous production functions of $\bar{x}$ and $\bar{y}$ are characterized by the unit isoquants illustrated in Figure 2. As shown in the diagram, $\bar{x}$ is uniformly x-intensive, and $\bar{y}$ is y-intensive. An initial input-price ratio is given by the slope of ae, and the corresponding equilibrium input-points are f and g respectively. Note that the physical units of $\bar{x}$ and $\bar{y}$ were defined in such a way as to make both unit isoquants tangential to ae. The unit cost and price of the two products measured in terms of input x is $0a$. (Note that ae is nothing but a constant-cost line corresponding to the level of output of one unit.) Suppose that the input x becomes relatively twice as expensive, the new relative input-price ratio being represented by the slope of the parallel lines passing through b and c. In terms of the input x, $0c$ is the new price of $\bar{x}$ and $0b$ is the new price of $\bar{y}$. Both products have become less expensive (in terms of input x), but the output $\bar{x}$ is now relatively more expensive. As the reader may verify, this relative cheapening of $\bar{y}$ would have occurred with a more expensive x for any initial and terminal relative input-price ratio, provided that there are no factor reversals, as we have assumed. We thus get for our case S (that is, $\bar{x}$ relatively x-intensive) a uniform relation between input prices R and output prices $\bar{R}$ shown by the line SS in Figure 3-a. If we relabel the axes in Figure 2, from x to y and from y

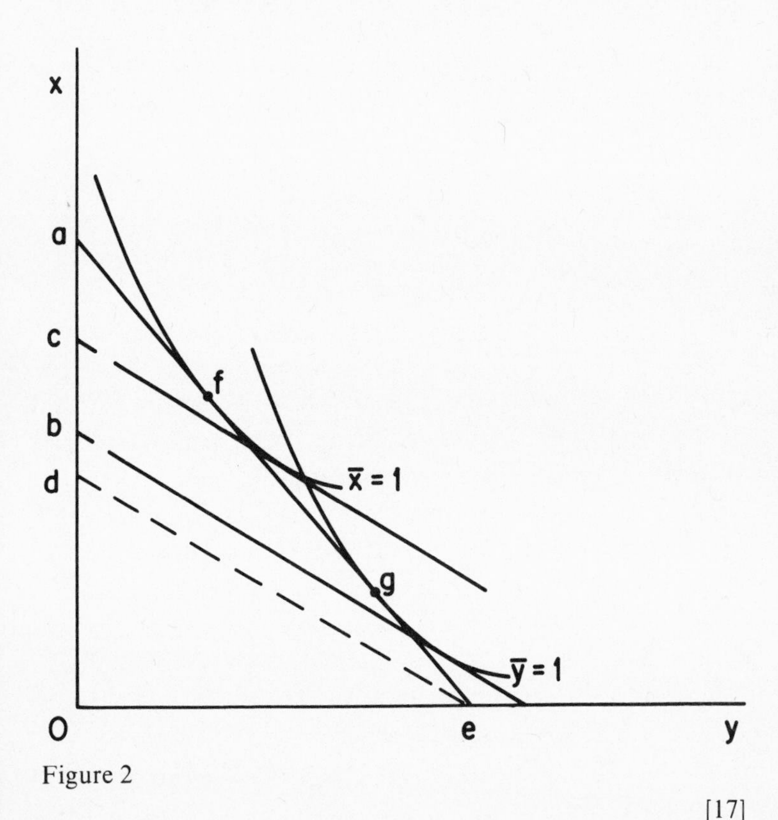

Figure 2

to x, we immediately obtain a situation descriptive of the Z-case and a uniform relation between R and $\bar{R}$ illustrated by the uniformly declining contour ZZ in Figure 3-b.

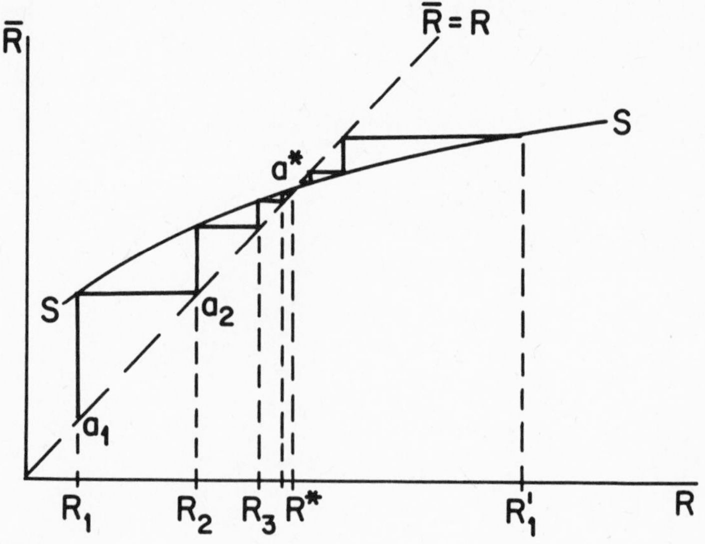

Figure 3-a

Of paramount importance for our analysis is another characteristic of the SS and ZZ contours, also recorded in Figures 3-a and 3-b but not yet proved—namely, that the absolute value of the contour elasticities must be smaller than 1. If we reconsider Figure 2, which underlies the construction of the SS contour in Figure 3-a, we observe that while in our construction the relative input price $R(= p_y/p_x)$ dropped to one-half the initial price ratio (note that $0d$ is one half of $0a$ in Figure 2), the product-price ratio $\bar{R}(= p_{\bar{y}}/p_x)$ declined from $\bar{R}_0 = 1$ only to $\bar{R}_1 = 0b/0c$, which is larger than one half —that is, $\bar{R}_1 > 1/2$. The latter inequality again is a necessary one, whatever the position of the unit isoquants, given the assumptions that there are no factor reversals and that the isoquants are smooth and convex. This conclusion is best seen from the fact that only in the degenerate case —not permitted by our assumptions—where *f* coincides with *a* and *g* with *e* and where both isoquants have kinks

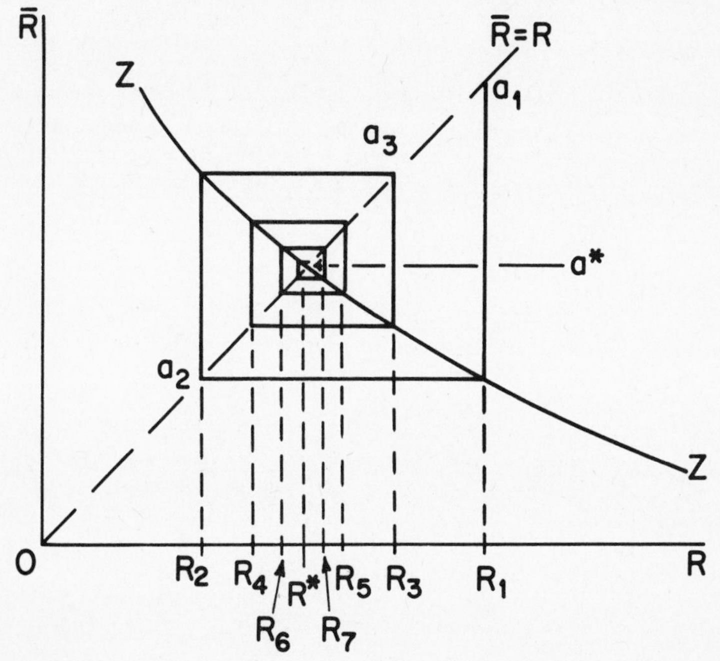

Figure 3-b

at these points, would R and $\bar{R}$ change in proportion. A perfectly analogous set of arguments, with axes in Figure 2 again relabeled, leads to the conclusion that in the Z-case doubling of R cannot reduce $\bar{R}$ by as much as, or more than, 50 per cent.

Because relative input prices R can vary between zero and plus infinity, the SS and ZZ lines are defined for this entire range; and because their elasticities must be less than 1 in absolute value, they can (and must) intersect the first diagonal ($\bar{R} = R$) only once. In other words, there can be no less and no more than one level of R—to be referred to hereafter as R^*—for which relative input and output prices are equal, that is, $\bar{R}^* = R^*$.

Let us now consider the variation of relative input and output prices as we move from A_0—recalling Figure 1—to higher T-contours along an efficient path A. The data of the problem uniquely determine the locus T_1, and on that locus we have selected point A_1 as the first point of our efficient path. Recalling that we are in the S-case, the corresponding relative-price situation is illustrated by Figure 3-a. The relative prices of outputs, $\bar{R}$ (slope of T_1 at A_1 in Figure 1), and of inputs, R (corresponding to point A_1 in Figure 1), are equal at the level R_1 ($= R_1$); recall that R and $\bar{R}$ must be equal for intertemporal efficiency. Thus we obtain the point a_1 in Figure 3-a corresponding to A_1 in Figure 1. But as we have shown earlier in this chapter, the input-price ratio R_1 must lead to an output-price ratio $\bar{R}_2$, given by the SS line. $\bar{R}_2$ in turn must equal R_2, and thus we get—as indicated by the solid step-function in Figure 3-a—a new point a_2 reflecting the efficient relative prices at A_2 in Figure 1. In a similar manner we get points a_3, a_4, . . . , corresponding to the subsequent points of the efficient path A. After an infinite number of steps—of course, providing that the A-path permits of an infinite number of points[10]—the point a^* in Figure 3-a, corresponding to $\bar{R}^* = R^*$, is reached. A similar construction and convergence per-

[10] As we will show later, the A-path will most often end after a finite number of steps, or points, such as A in Figure 1; consequently only a portion of the step function in Figure 3-a may have a real significance. Actually, for each T_1 in Figure 1, only one of the infinity of possible levels of initial relative prices R_1 will be found to permit of an infinite number of steps.

tains to an initial point a to the right of a^*. If the initial marginal rates of substitution and transformation at A_1 are exactly equal to R_1^*, of course, that relative price ratio will never change as we move along an efficient path A. Such paths with invariant $R = R^*$ will be our concern in Chapter V.

Only a few words need now be said about the Z-case, whose price variation associated with an efficient path A is illustrated in Figure 3-b. Here, as shown in the diagram, the convergence to R^* from an initial relative price level R takes the form of a cobweb function. And thus the consecutive points a_i alternate from right to left of a^*. As in the S-case, the convergence is guaranteed because the elasticity of the contour relating $\bar{R}$ to R is less than unity in absolute value. It will again take an infinite number of steps to reach R^* from any $R_1 \neq R^*$, while an initial $R_1 = R^*$ will be perpetuated for the entire length of an efficient path A (whether finite or infinite).

V. The steady-price situation and the maximal Von Neumann path

We must now consider all the possible efficient paths characterized by R^* (as defined in the preceding chapter) and show the derivation of one of these paths—generally referred to as the Von Neumann path or ray—which will be of central importance for the rest of our analysis.

Suppose that in Figure 4 the slope of line *ab* in the *x*-*y* plane represents the relative price ratio $R^* = \bar{R}^*$ derived in Chapter IV. For prescribed technologies of *x* and *y*, any of the points on *ab* could be an efficient point (such as A_1 in Figure 1) on T_1, characterized by the marginal rates of substitution and transformation $R^* = \bar{R}^*$, provided that the initial endowment point A_0 were correspondingly selected. Now consider one such point *e* on *ab*. It defines a production box and an efficiency locus or contract curve (not shown in the figure) and, corresponding to that contract curve, a production possibility *tt* such as t_2 in Figure 1. Point *i* is a point on the contract curve $0e$ corresponding to factor proportions reflected by $0c$ and $0f$ (note that we are again in the *S*-situation), which in turn are uniquely determined by the relative input prices R^*. Since units of measurement are selected in such a way as to make distances reflect approximately the levels of output, relatively little of $\bar{x}$ and a good deal of $\bar{y}$ are being produced at point *i*—and this is shown also by the point *e′* on *tt*, which uniquely corresponds to *i*. As required, the marginal rate of transformation at *e′* also equals $R^* = \bar{R}^*$. Point *e′* is now the next point on an efficient expansion path (comparable to A_2 in Figure 1), that path being defined by R^* and the initial point *e*.

With unchanged R^* and, thus, input proportions of $\bar{x}$ and $\bar{y}$, all other points such as *e′* can now be derived by sliding a point such as *e* along *ab*, leaving the slopes of such rays as 0*i* and *ei* unchanged, and recording for each point such as *i*—that is, 0, *h*, *g*, and *c* in Figure 4—the corresponding outputs, thus tracing a locus of effi-

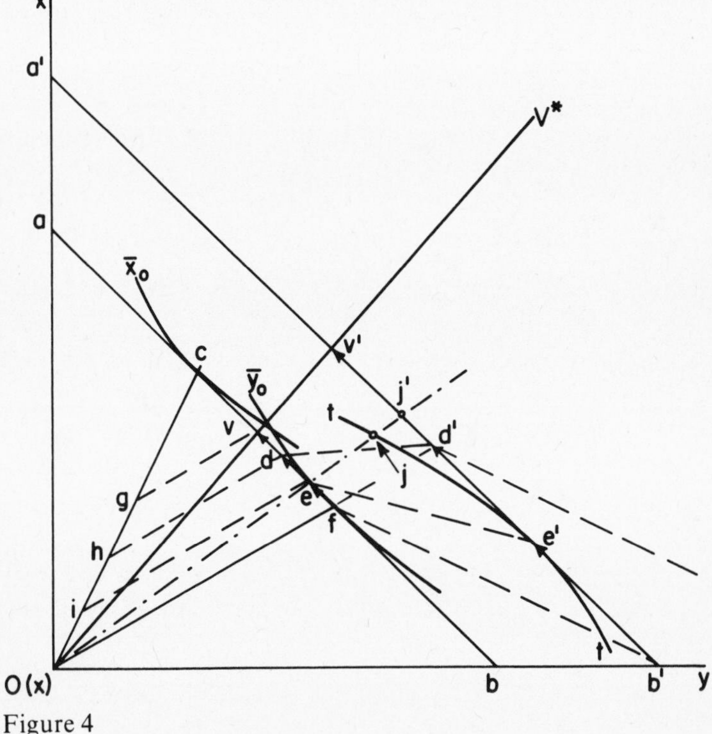

Figure 4

cient next points (such as e'). The technologies are characterized by the isoquants $\bar{x}_0$ and $\bar{y}_0$ respectively. Thus the range of points on ab leading to efficient next points (such as e') is only the stretch cf, because, as is apparent from the tangency of the two isoquants to ab, when productive resources are represented by f (by c), the efficient point of resource allocation on the contract curve must be 0 (must be c) thus leading to an output of only $\bar{y}$ (only $\bar{x}$).

We know that at all the new, second-stage output points such as a', v', d', e', and b', relative prices again must be $R^* = \bar{R}^*$. Moreover, with constant relative input and output prices and a constant value of total inputs, with only composition of output changing, the value of output (in terms of a product or a factor) must be constant under fully competitive conditions; therefore we know that the locus $a'b'$ must be a straight line parallel to ab. A third-generation locus could now be constructed for all points such as A_3 in Figure 1, characterized by $R^* = \bar{R}^*$. For example, as the reader will easily verify from the construction, point d' on $a'b'$ would now become the extremity of the admissible range for efficient points on a hypothetical $a''b''$ line, and so on.

The reader will also find it easy to verify that in the Z-case (with axes relabeled from x to y and from y to x), a line such as $a'b'$ again would be defined and have analogous properties, with one important exception: a movement along ab in one direction (say, northwest) would now correspond to a movement on $a'b'$ in the opposite direction (southwest). The output point a' would now correspond to resource availability at f, because in that situation and $R = R^*$ only $\bar{y}$ could be produced efficiently.

It is apparent from the construction—whether for the S-case or the Z-case—that for the situation described in

Figure 4 there will be one and only one point on *ab*, such as *v*, leading in the next efficient step to an output point, such as *v*′, characterized by outputs proportional to those at *v*. That there can be only one such point is immediately apparent for the *Z*-case from the fact that the movements of corresponding points along *ab* and *a*′*b*′ are in opposite directions. For the *S*-case the result follows from the fact inherent in the construction that the movements along *ab* and *a*′*b*′, while in the same direction, are of uniformly different angular speed. (Note that while a point such as *e*′ travels from *b*′ to *a*′, a point such as *e* must travel only from *f* to *c*.)

It is immediately apparent that instead of starting our analysis from the line *ab*, we could have started from *a*′*b*′ and derived a locus *a*″*b*″. Similarly, we could have derived from *v*′ a point *v*″, which would also have the proportionality properties just established for *v*′; a similar procedure would have led from *v*″ to a proportional *v*‴, and so forth. The ray 0*vv*′, or V^*, thus is an efficient expansion path characterized by constant relative prices $R^* = \bar{R}^*$ and proportionality of outputs. As we have shown in this chapter, the path is unique for $R^* = \bar{R}^*$; but because—as we have seen in the preceding chapter—R^* is unique for a prescribed set of technologies (relations) (1) and (2), the path V^* (proportional, efficient, and associated with constant R^*) is also unique for the prescribed technologies. To be on that path in period 1 and to stay on it indefinitely, it is necessary that the locus T_1 (see Figure 1), at the point where V^* intersects it, have the slope $\bar{R}^*$. But as the reader may want to verify through a construction of the type shown here, this is possible only if the initial endowment point A_0 (see Figure 1) also lies on V^*.

The ray of proportional and efficient growth is the so-called *Von Neumann ray* or *path*. It is the central concept of all the subsequent chapters of this study. The price ratio $R^* = \bar{R}^*$, uniquely associated with V^*, is often referred to as the *Von Neumann price ratio*.

Thus far we have shown that for a prescribed set of technologies there will be a unique path V^* which is intertemporally efficient, proportional, and associated with constant marginal rates of transformation and substitution $R^* = \bar{R}^*$. The first question we may ask is: Are there other paths, efficient and proportional, but associated with R's other than R^* and therefore (see Chapter IV) of necessity with R's that are changing? The answer is: Obviously, there cannot be any such paths, because with changing R's an efficient path cannot indefinitely be proportional. (The reader may verify this, or wait for Chapter VII, where the proposition is proven rigorously. At this point let it only be noted that with changing R's the similar production boxes generated by consecutive points of a proportional ray would have to have similar contract curves, and, at the same time, allocation points such as g in Figure 4 would have to travel to "dissimilar" positions; but this contradicts the original postulate of proportionality of the output points.) We thus can conclude that V^* is the only efficient proportional path corresponding to prescribed technologies, the constancy of R being its implied characteristic rather than part of its definition.

Of greater importance are the questions whether there may be intertemporally inefficient proportional paths and, if so, how they compare with V^* in respect of the speed at which one can move along them. Both questions can be answered at once by looking again at Figure 4.

Consider, for example, the ray $0ej'$ and suppose that point e is a point on an expansion path. We know already from our previous discussion that the points attainable from e in the next period are all points on tt (including e', which was important to us earlier in this chapter). Thus there is a point j on tt involving outputs proportional to those at e. And similarly, we could obtain a third-period point on the proportional ray at the same relative distance from j as is j from e, and so forth. Obviously, the path would not be intertemporally efficient, because all the marginal rates of substitution R along it (equal among themselves) would be different from the marginal rates of transformation $\overline{R}$ (also equal among themselves); this is apparent from Figure 4.

The important conclusion is that point j—or any other point similarly obtained for any other ray through the origin excepting V^*—must fall below $a'b'$. This conclusion immediately follows from the parallelism of aa and $a'b'$, the tangency of loci such as tt to $a'b'$, and the concavity of these loci. And consequently we can conclude that while there is an infinite number of proportional time paths other than V^*, not only are all such paths intertemporally inefficient, but also the movement along them proceeds at a smaller percentage rate than along V^*.

We may refer to the maximal rate of growth, corresponding to a movement along V^*, as r^*. In terms of the construction of Figure 4 it can be expressed as equal to the ratio of segments $vv'/0v$, or as $0v'0v - 1$.[11]

[11] Although this is of lesser analytical importance for us than for other, more mathematical, studies of the present subject, it should be noted that r^* can also be given another meaning. It can be interpreted as the rate of interest associated with the intertemporal growth situation corresponding to V^*. More specifically, under fully competitive conditions, a dollar in one period can be transformed into a dollar times $(1 + r^*)$ in the next period. Note that if it were not so temporarily, profitable arbitrage among borrowing, lending, and producing would eventually have to lead to such a result.

VI. "Smooth" and "zigzag" efficient paths distinguished

Having compared in the preceding chapter the Von Neumann path with inefficient proportional paths, we may now ignore the intertemporally inefficient situations and concentrate henceforth only on the efficient paths. Our first task is to spell out explicitly the distinction between growth paths of the *S*-type and those of the *Z*-type, using the results of Chapters III, IV, and V.

The two basic patterns of the efficient growth paths, *S*-type and *Z*-type, are illustrated in Figures 5-a and 5-b. Turning first to Figure 5-a, we recognize in A^* the path defined by T_1, a steady-price ratio $R^* = \bar{R}^*$, and technologies relatively intensive in the input which they are producing as output. As is apparent from the analysis in Chapter V, the path A^*—if V^* were drawn in the diagram—would fall entirely to one side of V^*, and, in general, reveal a rather regular pattern. From Chapter IV we know that efficient paths other than the steady-price path must, for any finite number of periods, have either $R = \bar{R} > R^* = \bar{R}^*$ or $R = \bar{R} < R^* = \bar{R}^*$. From this requirement and from the convexity of the efficient frontiers T_i it follows that all points of another efficient path, such as A or A', must be to one side of A^*. More generally, when we observe from Figure 3-a that for the *S*-case a path starting with a higher (lower) $R = \bar{R}$ than another path will always have a higher (lower) $R = \bar{R}$ for any finite number of periods, and when we recall the convexity of the T_i's, it follows that two S-paths (of course, corresponding to the same initial conditions A_0 and the same technologies) can never intersect.

The Z-case illustrated in Figure 5-b is quite different. A^* again is defined by the constant price-ratio $R^* = \bar{R}^*$; this time, however, unless $A^* = V^*$, A^* will reveal a zigzag pattern—as is easily ascertained from the analysis of Chapter V—its points alternating between one and the other side of V^*. (Note that when the axes in Figure 4 are relabeled to conform to the requirements of the Z-situation, the steady-price point corresponding to, say, d on ab would be found on $a'b'$ northwest of v'.) Another

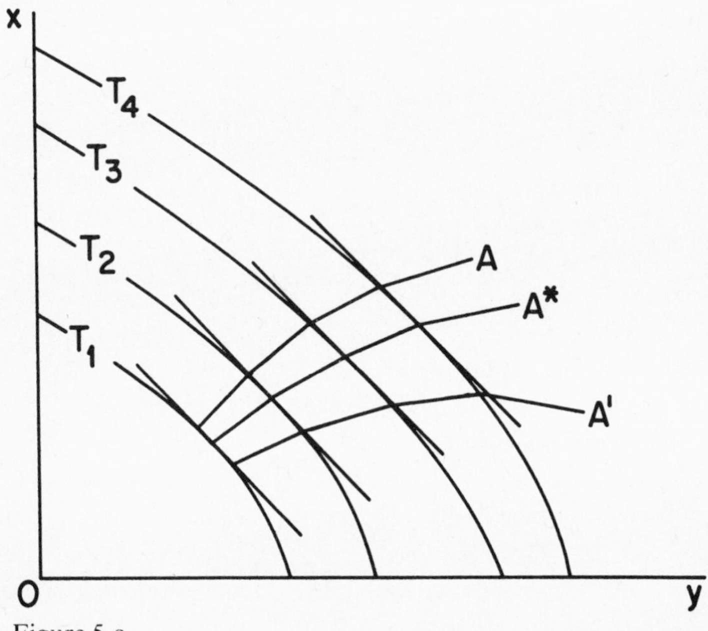

Figure 5-a

path, such as A in Figure 5-b, will zigzag itself around the already zigzagging path A^*. This fact follows from the convexity of the T_i frontiers and the alternating pattern of $R = \bar{R}$ shown in Figure 3-b. Moreover, the cobweb construction in Figure 3-b can be used in showing easily that if a path's initial price-point, such as a_1, is to the left of a_1 (on the first diagonal), the subsequent a_i points would all have to lie closer to a^* than the corresponding original points actually drawn in the diagram. And consequently it follows—recalling again the convexity of the T_i's—that a path in Figure 5-b originating on T_1 between (outside) A^* and A would have to remain between (outside) A^* and A. Such a path is illustrated, without actually being traced, by the small circles on the T-frontiers. Clearly, the result just obtained corresponds to the non-

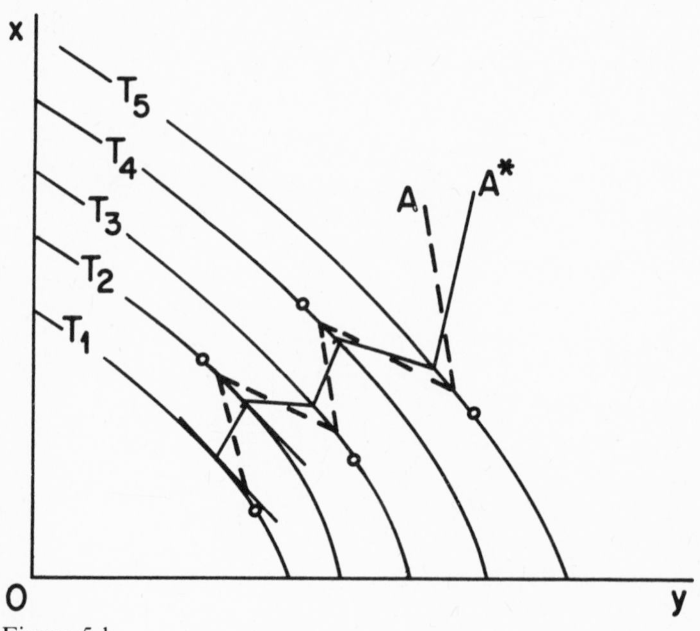

Figure 5-b

intersection condition obtained for the S-case. Even here, however, although the zigzagging implies intersection at each period, the nonintersection condition is fulfilled in the sense that two paths can never go through the same point. What is just about the same thing—and this will be useful to us later—the two paths formed for each single path A by connecting all even- and all odd-dated points respectively can never intersect.

VII. Some basic properties of efficient paths and efficient path points

Before proceeding further, we should prove or spell out certain basic properties of the efficient paths.[12] A large number of theorems could be derived here; however, we will concentrate only on those that will subsequently be useful to us in our analysis of efficient long-range development patterns and, in particular, of the so-called turnpike theorem. Most of the analysis below is conducted in the context of the *S*-case and proofs or results for the *Z*-case are only briefly indicated or referred to the reader as an exercise.

First we must note that for prescribed technologies and arbitrary initial conditions A_0 an infinite number of efficient paths, each corresponding to a given efficient price ratio $R = \overline{R}$, can pass through a given point A_i in the x-y plane. Thus the first question we can ask is: What is the relation between the path in the immediate vicinity of A_i—that is, the segments $A_{i-1}A_i$, and A_iA_{i+1}—and the marginal rates R? (Henceforth we can omit the expression $R = \overline{R}$, it being understood that for an intertempo-

[12]To my best knowledge this has not been done elsewhere in the literature, probably because knowledge of the properties was not required as an input into the proof of the turnpike theorem.

rally efficient path the two R's must be always equal.) The easily demonstrable answer is as follows:

Conclusion I: Given a clockwise rotation of the R-line (the line whose slope reflects R_i), the segments $A_{i-1}A_i$ and A_iA_{i+1} will rotate around A_i clockwise in the S-case (counterclockwise in the Z-case) and vice versa for the opposite rotation of the R-line.

Figure 6 shows, with minor alterations, the box diagram already familiar from Chapter III. It will be recalled that the coordinates of A_{i+1} are $x = a$ and $y = b$ (in the S-case illustrated in the diagram), resulting from the previous (ith) period's allocation of resources at point c (on the contract curve $0A_i$). Now if with the same resources, given by A_i, the R-line is to rotate counterclockwise (as indicated by the arrow), the marginal rates of substitution in both industries must change in the corresponding manner (x must become relatively more expensive). But on the assumption of linear-homogeneous technologies, this change involves a movement along the contract curve to the northeast of point c; that is, it in-

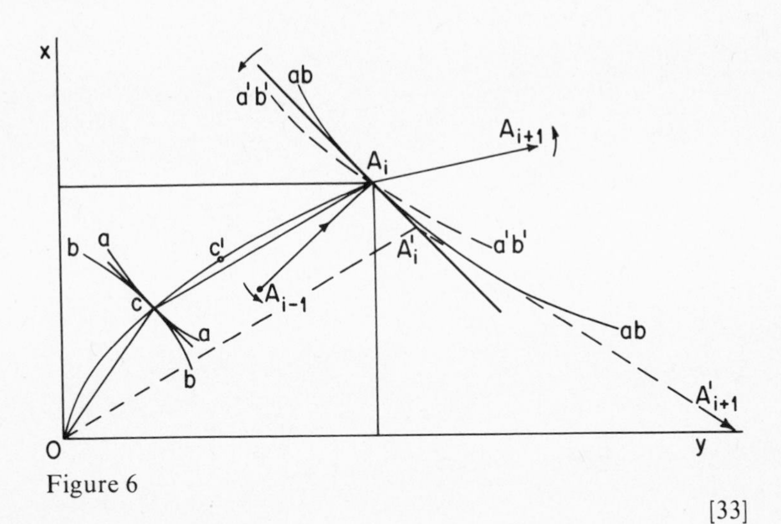

Figure 6

volves an increase in the output of x and a decline in the output of y. In other words, as indicated by the arrow, the segment A_iA_{i+1} will rotate counterclockwise. It is easily seen—again by relabeling the axes—that in the Z-case the opposite rotation will be found for A_iA_{i+1}.

To understand the rotation of $A_{i-1}A_i$, recall that to a point such as A_{i+1} lead all points of a preceding period, such as A_i, along the "Scitovsky-isoquant" *ab-ab*. A point on that locus southeast of A_i in Figure 6 will correspond to a flatter R-line (x more expensive) at the new A; but with x more expensive as an input, the x-intensive product—that is, $\bar{x}$ in the S-case—must become relatively more expensive. And thus a clockwise movement of the segment of the efficient path (such as here considered for a connection between *ab-ab* and A_{i+1}) can be associated with a clockwise movement of the R-line passing through the terminal point of the segment, as shown by the arrow at A_{i-1}.

Another useful proposition can be derived regarding the rotation of adjacent segments of an efficient path resulting from shifts of A_i.

Conclusion II: With unchanged R, any shift of A_i to a position of an increased x/y ratio will rotate the A segments $A_{i-1}A_i$ and A_1A_{i+1} counterclockwise around A_i in the S-case (clockwise in the Z-case); the opposite results hold for movements of A_i to lower x/y ratios.

A third conclusion is obvious from the second.

Conclusion III: With no change in R and the x/y ratio, shifts in A_i leave unchanged the slopes of $A_{i-1}A_i$ and A_iA_{i+1}.

To show Conclusions II and III valid—recalling that in our linear-homogeneous situation only the input and output ratios are significant—the point A_i' can be taken as fully characteristic of a movement of A_i to a lower x/y ratio. As indicated by the broken line $0A'_i$, parallel to cA_i on account of a constant R, productive resources given by A'_i and used efficiently with input prices R will not permit any production of x. We have thus the point A'_{i+1} in the diagram. Because of the complete linearity of the construction, as the reader may verify, the trajectory between A_{i+1} and A'_{i+1} is covered by a hypothetical traveling point in percentages of distance equal to those traveled by the corresponding hypothetical point between A_i and A'_i. And consequently we arrive at Conclusion II regarding reductions of the x/y ratio. An analogous argument can be used, again for the S-case, in respect of increased x/y ratios. The proofs of Conclusion II for the Z-case are even more straightforward; indeed, with relabeled axes, a movement of A_i southeast must move A_iA_{i+1} counterclockwise, any considerations of comparative distances covered now being irrelevant because the movements are in opposite directions.

Of course, if increased x/y ratios make segments such as A_iA_{i+1} rotate in one direction and reduced x/y ratios produce rotation in the other direction movements of A_i with no change in the x/y ratio will produce no rotation.

The conclusions regarding the rotation of the (backward) segment $A_{i-1}A_i$ with shifts of A_i are easily obtained by reversing this procedure. If we consider point A_{i+1} as the pivotal point and shift it, along the straight trajectory $A_{i+1}A'_{i+1}$, all the way to A'_{i+1}, the preceding point A_i shifts only to A'_i, and thus the nature of the (backward) rotation A_iA_{i+1} around A_{i+1} is established for shifts in the S-case to lower x/y ratios. A similar set of arguments is applicable to all other relevant alternatives. It may be useful to recall that with the same relative input prices R_0, along any efficient path, the output prices $\bar{R}_0$ (different from, or equal to, R_0) must also be the same.

Our next conclusion, which will be useful in the subsequent chapter, concerns the Scitovsky-type isoquants known to us already from Chapter III. We find such a locus in Figure 6 marked as *ab-ab*; we recall that it indicates the minimum combinations of inputs of x and y required to produce constant quantities of $\bar{x} = a$ and $\bar{y} = b$ (the coordinates of A_{i+1}). By changing scales along the x and y axes in a proportional manner multiplying the present scales by the same arbitrary number k and recalling the linear homogeneity of the two production functions, we realize that the contour *ab-ab* is representative of a linear homogeneous (homothetic) family of similar contours, each having the property that it represents the minimum inputs necessary to produce constant amounts of the two outputs $\bar{x} = ka$ and $\bar{y} = kb$ (that is, outputs along a ray defined by 0 and A_{i+1}).

Corresponding to point c' on the contract curve in Figure 6 and to outputs $\bar{x} = a'$ and $\bar{y} = b'$, such that $a/b < a'/b'$, we find another Scitovsky-type isoquant, $a'b'$-$a'b'$. The latter also is representative of a homogeneous family corresponding to outputs $\bar{x} = k'a'$ and $\bar{y} = k'b'$. The important result here is that the new Scitovsky isoquant at A_i (and hence all other loci of the same family at points of the ray through 0 and A_i) is flatter than *ab-ab*. This is a necessary result, with linear-homogeneous production functions, whenever $a/b < a'b'$, following from the fact that along the contract curve, with homogeneous technologies, the marginal rates of substitution must be uniformly changing (in one direction or the other, depending on whether we are in the

S- or the Z-situation) as we move from 0 to A_i, and from the fact that the slope of the Scitovsky isoquant at A_i must be the same as the marginal rates of substitution for the corresponding allocation of productive resources (the corresponding point c). Using a convenient wording, we may sum up this finding as our fourth conclusion.

Conclusion IV: In the S-case (Z-case), a Scitovsky-type family of isoquants defined by two linear-homogeneous technologies employing x and y and by a constant ratio of outputs $\bar{x}/\bar{y} = a/b$ will be uniformly x-intensive compared to another Scitovsky-type family of isoquants defined by the same technologies and a ratio of outputs $\bar{x}/\bar{y} = a'/b' > (<) a/b$.

Our next and last "useful" conclusion is derived from Conclusions I, II, and III, in conjunction with the results we obtained in Chapter IV for variations in R and $\bar{R}$ along an efficient path.

Conclusion V: An efficient path in the S-case, or a path formed by every other point of an efficient path in the Z-case, cannot intersect a ray through the origin more than twice.

Leaving aside the paths corresponding to R^*, which we studied in Chapter V and which, obviously, can intersect a ray through the origin at most once, let us concentrate on the paths with variable R's. We will produce the desired proofs for the S-case, leaving the task of doing likewise for the Z-case to the reader. First, it will be observed (for case S) that if $R \neq R^*$, R_i must be uniformly increasing or declining (depending on its position relative to R^*) with increasing and finite i.

Next, consider in Figure 7 the hypothetical portion of a path A_i through A_{i+3}, with the R-lines, as required, uniformly becoming steeper (R as defined earlier is increasing). The path intersects (or crosses) three times the ray 00′. Starting from A_{i+1}, and considering the movement in R, we find that there is nothing in steps $A_{i+1}A_{i+2}$ and $A_{i+2}A_{i+3}$ inconsistent with Conclusions I through III; two intersections of the ray 00′ are thus possible. The segment A_iA_{i+1}, however, is inconsistent with Conclusions I and II combined. Note that we have shifted, proceeding along that segment, to an increased relative *y*-

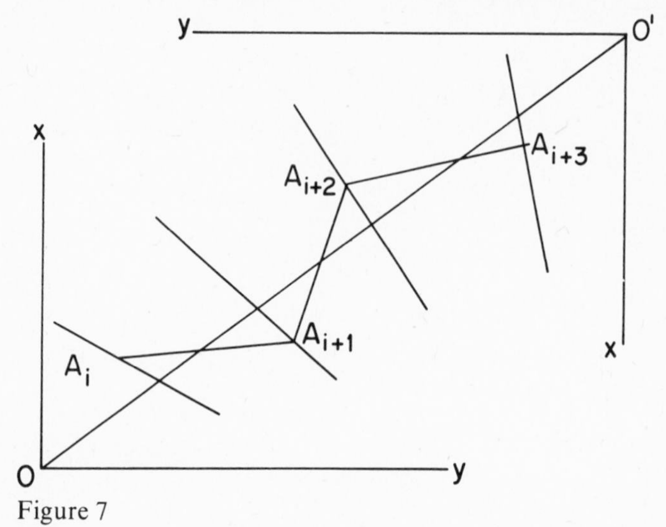

Figure 7

intensity and the R-line has become steeper; on both accounts, $A_{i+1}A_{i+2}$ should have rotated clockwise, relative to A_iA_{i+1}, around A_{i+1}. But in the incorrect representation in Figure 7 it did just the opposite. By turning the diagram by 180 degrees, we can obtain the same result for a flattening R-line. It will also be noted that the proof is equally valid if the crossing of 00′ does not take place in consecutive steps as in Figure 7; the important thing is that whatever the number of steps, there must be a uniform relation between the R_i's for increasing i's.

VIII. Efficient funnels and long-range growth

In this and most of the subsequent chapters we will study the long-range properties of the efficient paths; more specifically, we will learn more about the efficient trajectories that bring the economy from its initial production possibility T_1 to a terminal efficient locus (or frontier) T_N at time N. Most of the interesting results pertain to all, rather than to only one or some, efficient paths leading from T_1 to T_N, and consequently it is convenient to study all such paths together. For that purpose, let us define as an *efficient funnel*, or simply "funnel," $F(N)$, the collection of *all* efficient paths leading from T_1 to T_N.[13]

In Figure 8, for example (note that as drawn it represents the S-case), we find as the simplest possible illustration the funnel $F(2)$, defined by the entirety of T_2, and the segment of T_1 falling between the two contours $f(-1)$ and $f'(-1)$. As indicated in the diagram, these two contours are obtained as loci of points of tangency between the T_i's and isoquants of the two production functions, the isoquants of $\bar{x}$ leading to $f'(-1)$ and those of $\bar{y}$ to $f(-1)$. They are also loci of points of all conceivable funnels, for $N = 2, 3, \ldots, \infty$, preceding by one period

[13] We recall that T_1 is defined by the initial endowment A_0 and the production functions for $\bar{x}$ and $\bar{y}$.

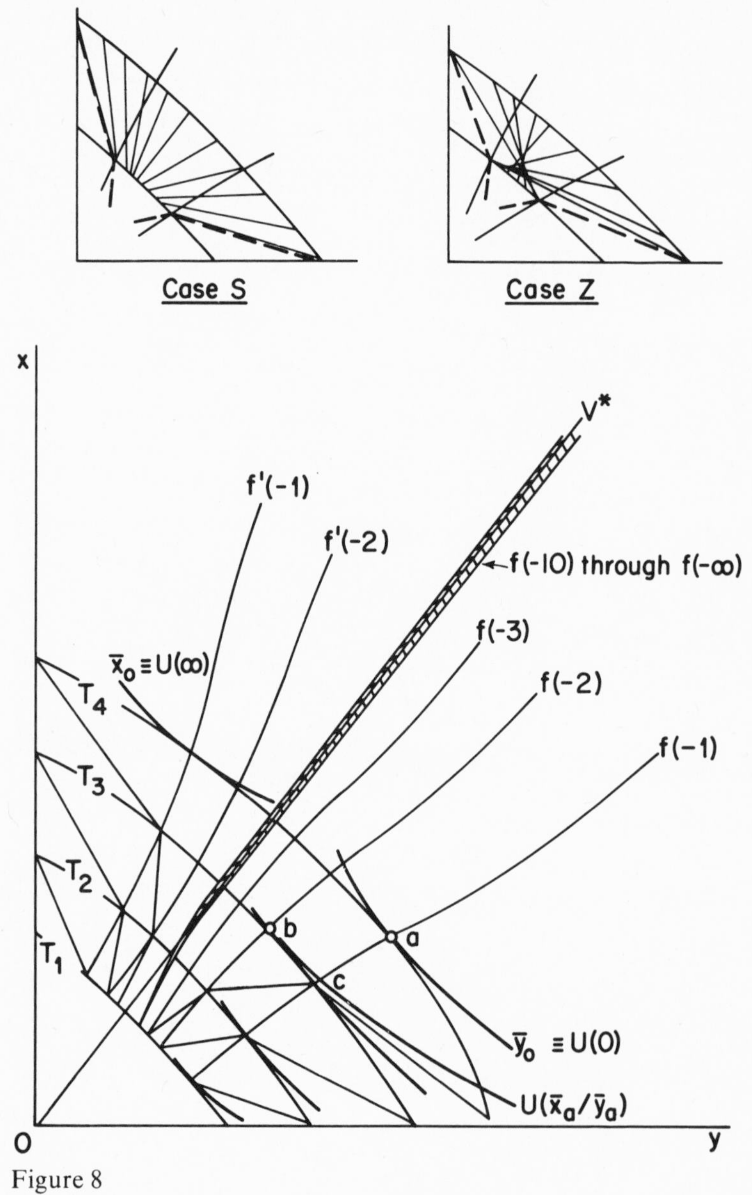
Case S
Case Z
x
V*
f'(-1)
f'(-2)
f(-10) through f(-∞)
f(-3)
f(-2)
f(-1)
x̄₀ ≡ U(∞)
T4
T3
T2
T1
b
a
c
ȳ₀ ≡ U(0)
U(x̄a/ȳa)
O
y

Figure 8

the terminal T_N. This is why our first funnel $F(2)$ is defined on T_1 by the intersections with $f(-1)$ and $f'(-1)$. In Figure 8 we also find loci $f(-2)$ and $f'(-2)$, $f(-3)$ and $f'(-3)$, ... Analogously to $f(-1)$ and $f'(-1)$ they are defined as loci on all conceivable funnels, preceding by 2, 3, ... periods the terminal T_N.

The construction of the $f(-1)$ loci should be obvious to the reader who has gone through the preceding seven chapters. For example, at point a in the diagram, R is equal to $\overline{R}$ (the marginal rates of substitution and transformation are equal) with only $\overline{y}$ produced; the level of output of $\overline{y}$, as indicated in Figure 8, is $\overline{y}_0$. In other words, when the economy finds itself at point a in period 4, given the nature of T_4, it can produce efficiently (in the intertemporal sense) for the fifth period only at the y-maximum extremity of its production box, that is, only product $\overline{y}$.

It is convenient to think of the isoquants of $\overline{y}$ as special cases of the Scitovsky-type isoquants (see our discussion relative to Conclusion IV of the preceding chapter), to be designed by $U(0)$, corresponding to the output ratio $\overline{x}/\overline{y} = a/b = 0$. The a and b are the constants of proportionality used in the preceding chapter. $U(0)$ thus designates a whole family of homothetic isoquants; the isoquant defining and passing through point c is one of its members.

Now we know that the efficient path (again in the S-case) leading to point a must lead from a point on T_3 where a Scitovsky isoquant defined by point a—that is, $U(\overline{x}_a/\overline{y}_a)$—is tangential to T_3. Such a point is found at b on T_3; by our previous definition it belongs to $f(-2)$, and, what is most important, it must be to the left of and above point c. Since $\overline{x}_a/\overline{y}_a > 0$, this result is the immediate consequence of Conclusion IV in the preceding chapter. In simple terms, the Scitovsky isoquant at *b* must belong to a family uniformly more *x*-intensive than that of the isoquant determining point *c*; and this, coupled with the fact that the *T*-loci must be concave, gives us the result.

In a similar manner, all the points of $f'(-2)$ and $f(-2)$ are determined from points on the loci $f(-1)$. As just explained, the loci $f(-2)$ must be enclosed by the loci $f(-1)$. From the points of $f(-2)$ the loci $f(-3)$ are then determined, and so we go on, ad infinitum, the larger-number (in absolute value) *f*-loci always being enclosed by the lower-number ones. It is apparent from the construction of consecutive *f*-loci that the distance between *f* and f' can be made arbitrarily small at any finite T_N. On the limit, for any finite time horizon *N*, the two loci $f'(-\infty)$ and $f(-\infty)$ merge into one.

The actual funnel then can be obtained, say, for $N = 100$—that is, $F(100)$—by starting at the intersections of T_1 with $f(-99)$ and $f'(-99)$, normally of the order of some 10^{-40} of a degree apart, and then working one's way up, always jumping from an "inner" to the next outer *f*-locus as one proceeds from a lower to the next higher *T* frontier. In the absence of an electronic microscope, the complete funnel $F(100)$ would then normally appear for about the first ninety periods as a single line—coinciding most of the time with the shaded band around V^* in Figure 8—and then, opening up rapidly as an umbrella in the last ten years, reach at $N = 100$ the complete ninety-degree range of T_{100}. The nature of the coincidence—or near-coincidence—of the funnels with the Von Neumann path V^* will be our concern in some of the following chapters, and thus we will not elaborate on it here. Nor will we elaborate on the exact spot on T_1 that all the funnels have in common.

The one subject that remains is the Z-case. The analysis and construction of efficient funnels for that case are analogous to what we have just done for the S-case. Let us relabel the axes in Figure 8 from x to y and from y to x. Input points a and c and the locus $U(0)$ still correspond to a zero output of $\bar{x}$ and all resources allocated to the production of $\bar{y}$; these outputs of $\bar{y}$ are now to be found, however, in conformity with our analysis in Chapter VII, on the vertical axis. And thus we find the $f(-1)$ locus, corresponding to the intercepts of the T_i's with the relabeled vertical axis, south of V^*. This locus then leads to $f(-2)$ north of V^*, and so forth. If we decide, as we did before, to identify by a prime the f-loci corresponding to paths terminating along the x-axis (after relabeling), we ought to switch the odd-numbered labels from f to f' and from f' to f. On the basis of Conclusion IV, as the reader will easily verify, the two important conclusions still hold: the f-loci corresponding to further horizons will be necessarily enclosed by those corresponding to nearer horizons, and two loci $f'(-n)$ and $f(-n)$ must come arbitrarily near to each other at any T_N with a finite N for n sufficiently large.

In both situations, S and Z, the funnels here defined have the same property: they enclose all the corresponding efficient paths. Only the detailed period-to-period patterns are different, as is illustrated in the two drawings at the top of Figure 8.

IX. Other funnel properties and the turnpike theorem

In the preceding chapter we established probably the most important property of the efficient funnels: the fact that at a given T_i, such as T_{N-n} in Figure 9, a funnel $F(i + Q)$, such as $F(N - n + Q)$ in the diagram, will become arbitrarily thin (or slim) for Q sufficiently large. Two other important properties remain to be demonstrated: the location of the point on T_1 that all funnels have in common (such as b in Figure 9); and the near-coincidence of F—and thus of all individual paths it contains—with the Von Neumann path V^* in situations involving substantial numbers of periods—for example, $F(N)$ or $F(N + Q)$ in the diagram.

In most of this chapter we will be conducting our analysis in connection with the S-case. The reader may find it useful to translate, so to speak, all the arguments into the Z-environment, recalling that all the basic properties of efficient S-paths (see especially Chapter VII) are equally valid for paths formed of all odd or all even points of the Z-paths.

Now let us turn to Figure 9. Point c is the origin of A^*, the steady-price path (see Chapter V). Since R at all its points is equal to R^*, the slope of T_1 at c must be R^*. We know from our previous analysis that A^*, if it does not coincide with V^*, must diverge from V^* and disappear (be terminated) at an axis within a finite time span. The point b thus must be to the left of c because no F can be entirely below A^*. Now at point a (the intersection of V^* and T_1), given the convexity of T_1, R is less than R^*—that is, the tangency must be flatter. Thus by our Conclusion I, as discussed in Chapter VII, and recalling that the slope of V^* corresponds to R^*, the efficient path A originating at a must diverge upward from V^* at that point.

We noted in the preceding chapter that the two loci f

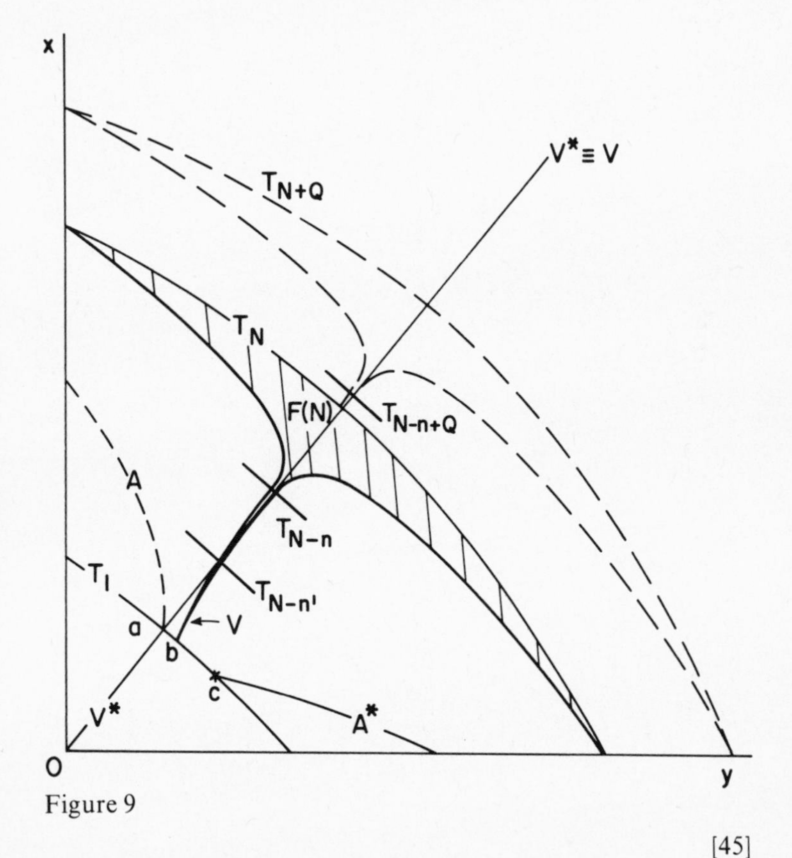

Figure 9

and f' merge into a single locus at any finite T_i, including T_1, as the terminal time horizon recedes to infinity; let us denote such a locus by $f^*(-\infty)$. Since $f(-n)$ and $f'(-n)$ are loci bounding funnels terminating in n periods, f^* must at any finite T_i, including T_1, coincide with $F(\infty)$. But obviously $F(\infty)$ must contain as one of its paths the path which we will denote by V and which coincides with V^* in infinity, that is, at the intersection between V^* and T_∞. In other words, V is the path asymptotic to, or identical with, V^*. Thus $F(\infty)$, $f^*(-\infty)$, and V all coincide for any finite time period, and their intersection with T_1 is point b, defined (but not yet fully located on T_1 in Figure 9) as the point common to all funnels on T_1.

It should be clear that point a on V^* and T_1 in the diagram could not also be point b, because A, the efficient path originating at a, diverges from V^* at a (as established above). But we know that the efficient path at b (wherever b may be) is the path identical with $F(\infty)$, and if A and $F(\infty)$ were to coincide at a, one of the two sides of the funnel $F(\infty)$—in fact, the lower side—would ultimately have to intersect V^* a second time (besides at a); and this is impossible. Note that the sides of any funnel are themselves formed by efficient paths and that an efficient S-path (or a path formed by every other point of a Z-path) cannot intersect V^* twice because this would be in violation of our Conclusion I, as discussed in Chapter VII, and of the fact demonstrated in Chapter IV, that for an S-path (or Z-path) every R (or every other R) must always be to one side of (either larger or smaller than) R^*. The same argument precludes A, the efficient path originating at a, from intersecting V^* a second time. But with A always to one side of V^*, b—the point common to all funnels including $F(\infty)$ on T_1—could not be northwest of a because this would involve intersections of efficient S-paths (paths formed by odd-numbered points of Z-paths) corresponding to the same initial T_1; we know that such intersections are impossible.

Consequently, b must be—as our intuition would have told us from the outset—between a and c on T_1. Of course, in the very special case where A^* and V^* coincide—that is, where T_1 at its intersection with V^* (which depends only on the technologies and not on the initial endowment) has the slope equal to R^*—a, b, and c will coincide.

Our observations in this chapter thus far make it relatively easy for us to substantiate our second proposition. Call e^i the angular distance measured along T_i in terms of degrees (and fractions thereof) between V^* and V. It can be shown that $e^i > e^{i+1}$ for all finite i. This follows from (i) the definition of V as a locus asymptotic to V^* and from (ii) the fact that V can cross any ray through the origin only once. Condition (ii) immediately follows from the fact that if V intersected a ray through the origin more than once it would have to do so at least three times, but this contradicts Conclusion V of Chapter VII.

But if V can get arbitrarily near V^* (in the sense just defined) with increasing i, and if $F(N)$ at T_i can become arbitrarily "slim" for N sufficiently large, then since $F(N)$ must contain V, what we have termed above the "near-coincidence" of V^* and $F(N)$ becomes quite evident. A more precise statement summarizing our findings leads to a generalization of the turnpike theorem.[14]

Theorem: Given any prescribed small angle $e > 0$ and any constant m, $0 < m < 1$, there will be a minimum

[14]The theorem was first enunciated by Dorfman, Samuelson, and Solow in *op. cit.*, chap. 12, with reference to a single efficient path.

number N_m^e such that $F(N_m^e)$ will be further away from V^* than e, measured in degrees along any T_i, no more than mN_m^e times, and when N is increased to any $\overline{N} > N_m^e$, the number of times $F(\overline{N})$ will be further away from V^* than e (again, in terms of an angular measure along T_i) will not exceed mN_m^e.

Of course, whatever the theorem says for a funnel must also hold regarding the individual paths it contains; it is in this respect of dealing with all paths simultaneously that the present theorem is a generalization.

The theorem may be obvious to—or have been already proved by—many readers who have worked their way up to this point. Nonetheless, I consider it useful to produce a proof of it in the subsequent chapter, not only to satisfy the usual requirement that theorems should be proved, but also, and perhaps primarily, because in the course of providing the proof we will gain some additional insights into the subject at hand.

Before leaving this chapter, however, we ought to make one further use of our Conclusions of Chapter VII in describing the general form of efficient funnels. As we have shown in our Conclusions, an efficient path cannot intersect a ray through the origin more than twice. A typical form of a funnel $F(N)$ with N large is thus that shown in Figure 9 (of course when c is on the other side of a, a more or less symmetrical pattern would emerge), where one limiting path of $F(n)$ (the upper one in the diagram) assumes each x/y ratio only once, and the other limiting path assumes most ratios once and some—not too different from that of V^*—twice. Only if b coincides with a and c are both limits of F single-valued with respect to a ray through the origin.

X. Proof of the turnpike theorem

Given our foregoing analysis—in particular that of the last two chapters—the proof of the theorem enunciated towards the end of Chapter IX is straightforward.[15] The first part of the theorem we have actually shown already; indeed, for an arbitrarily large fraction of the number of periods N, $F(N)$ can be made to fall within e of V^* provided that N is made to assume a large enough finite value. This follows from the convergences of V toward V^* and of F towards V explained in the preceding two chapters.

Thus it only remains to show that the number mN^e_m does not increase when N—the funnel horizon—is increased beyond N^e_m. Suppose that in Figure 9, for $F(N)$, the postulated proximity of V^* (within e) is attained between $T_{N-n'}$ and T_{N-n} (note that m is roughly $2/3$). If N is increased to $N + Q$, it is obvious that no additional periods where F is further away from V^* than e can appear in periods 1 through $N - n$. This follows from the fact that, as we have seen previously, the further-horizon

[15] The proof originally sketched by Dorfman, Samuelson, and Solow, *ibid.*, and later completed by Radner, *op. cit.*, and others proceeds along entirely different lines from what is offered here.

funnels must entirely "fit" into the nearer-horizon funnels for periods common to both. Actually, if anything, the number of periods where e is exceeded could be reduced since $F(N + Q)$ is slimmer than $F(N)$ below T_{N-n}.

Thus, as we move from $F(N)$ to $F(N + Q)$, the additional periods where F is further from V^* than e (e being an angular measure) can arise only at the "advanced" periods, beyond T_{N-n}. Now it should be clear from our discussion of Chapter VIII that if the loci $f(-n)$ and $f'(-n)$ (defined as loci of points on the T_i's n periods away from the terminal date of a funnel)—whether for case S or Z—were straight lines through the origin, by definition no additional points on $F(N + Q)$ further than e from V^* could be counted beyond the number n already counted for $F(N)$ north of T_{N-n}. It is equally clear that the loci f and f' (constructed in the same way as income-consumption-lines) would be straight lines through the origin if the T's were all straight and had the same slope. The essence of our proof is that in long-range situations where $N - n$ is large—and this is the context in which the turnpike theorem is always discussed and the only context in which the discussion makes any sense—the T-loci effectively come within an infinitesimal degree of being straight and parallel. Once we have completed our demonstration, the reader may find it interesting to verify that after fifty periods ($N - n = 50$)—for production functions x and y having about 10 per cent different factor proportions at R^*—the upper limit of the relative difference between the maximum and minimum slopes along T_{50} would be of the order of 10^{-100} and the slopes of all such T_i's, for $i \geq 50$, would be (again relatively) within 10^{-50} of R^*. I feel that such estimates entitle us to take the T_i's in the long run as parallel and having the slope of R^*.[16]

It suffices to draw a few lines in diagrams of the type of Figures 3-a or 3-b to see the nature of the long-run convergence of any initial R towards R^*. Only slightly less evident is the "double-order" convergence of the degree of straightness of the T-line (recall the exponent -100 as compared to the exponent -50 in the above numerical illustration). It is the result of how near any R, for any efficient path leading to the terminal T_N, comes to R^*, and of how small the initial range at T_1 becomes (the quasi-point b in Figure 9) for the conceivable efficient paths A leading as far as T_N. It will be noted that the smaller the initial range is, the smaller will also be the difference between the maximum and minimum initial R.

Some might want to argue that the convergence may be very slow if the line SS in Figure 3-a is almost parallel with, and near, the first diagonal. It will be observed first that this situation would call for extremely awkward production functions; but what is more important, it could not change the argument, because if the convergence is slow, then for a given e and m, in our theorem, N_m^e simply must become larger than what it would be when the convergence is fast.

[16] Actually the calculation on which these estimates, or similar ones, are based, while beyond the scope of this book, may be useful in all kinds of quantifications of Von Neumann growth situations, once the time-horizon has shifted to a sufficiently distant future.

XI. The case of identical technologies

Thus far we have dealt only with the cases S and Z—that is, the cases where, respectively, product $\bar{x}$ is relatively x-intensive and where $\bar{y}$ is relatively y-intensive. In this section we discuss briefly the situation where the two technologies are identical in the sense that identical factor proportions correspond (in competitive equilibrium) to identical relative input prices R.

In this situation, as is well known, for any resource endowments, both the contract curve in a production box and the production-possibility function are linear, and relative product prices $\bar{R}$ are a constant R_0 invariant with respect to relative input prices R. In a diagram such as Figure 3-a the price function (such as SS) becomes a horizontal line at the level $\bar{R} = R_0$, and thus $R^* = \overline{R^*} = R_0$. The x/y proportions corresponding to the Von Neumann ray—V^* in Figure 10—now are given by any isoquant typifying the two production functions—such as *ab-ab* in Figure 10—in conjunction with R^*. $R^* = \bar{R}^*$ is the slope of T_1 in the diagram and is uniquely determined, as before (in the cases S and Z), by A_0 and the two identical technologies. As indicated, points a, b, and c (defined in Chapter IX) now coincide, and b, which in the general situation was a "microscopic range" or a "quasi-point," now is a true point on T_1 and V^*. In other words, all efficient paths leading to any T_N, with $N > 1$, must pass through a. Moreover, because $R^* = \overline{R}^* = R_0$ is the only conceivable slope of T, and because there is only one conceivable Scitovsky isoquant (such as *ab-ab*, identical with typical isoquants of both $\bar{x}$ and $\bar{y}$), all efficient paths leading to T_N must coincide with V^* between T_1 and T_{N-1}. As shown in Figure 10, it is only at a', on T_{N-1}, that the infinity of paths leading to various points of T_N will branch out in a fanlike manner. The funnel $F(N)$ now is represented in the drawing in heavy lines defined by a, a', and the intercepts of T_N with the x and y axes. It may also be useful to observe that $0a'$ actually is the linear contract curve of the production box from which T_N is derived.

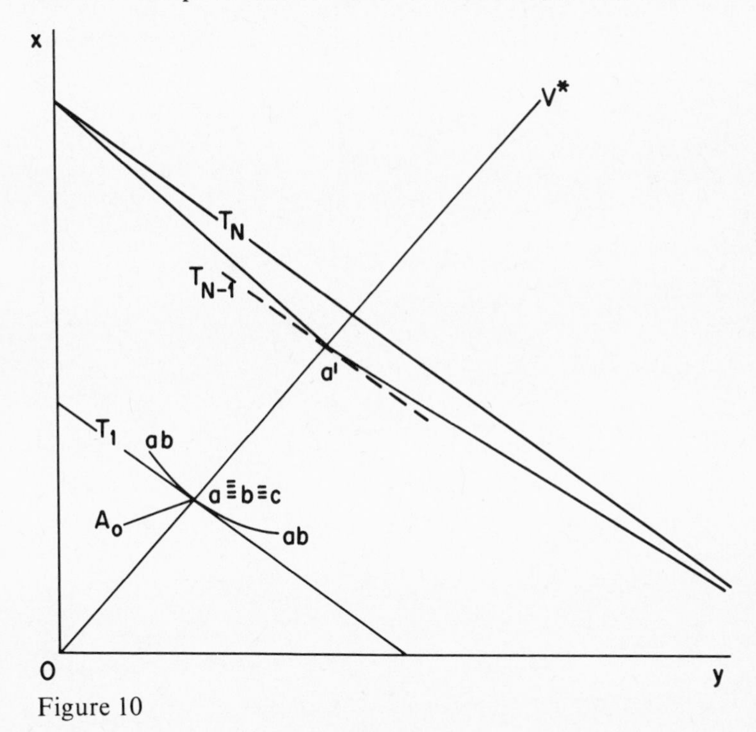

Figure 10

What we have just shown is actually the turnpike situation in its extreme version; immediately following period 0, any efficient path immediately proceeds to V^*, then remains on V^*—rather than very near it—and diverges to its final destination only in the last period. Moreover—and this is the essence of the turnpike theorem—shifting further into the future of the final time horizon (increasing N) does not augment the number (exactly, one) of periods wherein the efficient path is away from V^*; the term "away from" now is to be taken literally, rather than in its earlier meaning "not within e of V^*."

The situation just described is a basis for an intuitive proof of the more general turnpike theorem for cases S and Z. Suppose that instead of having identical technologies, we have technologies only slightly different. Because there is no reason to expect any discontinuities, this should only smoothen, so to speak, the corners of the heavily drawn pattern in Figure 10. A larger difference in technologies should produce more of such an effect. What is important, however, is that the funnel around V^* should never become too thick, say, at the level of $T_{N/2}$. This is so because as we know, a path far away from V^* with prices anywhere near R^*—and we know from Chapter IV that for $N/2$ sufficiently large R cannot be too different from R^*—must lead within very few periods to termination at one of the axes.

XII. The case of factor reversals

In order to study the case of factor reversals we will relax the assumption, made thus far, that the production functions of $\overline{x}$ and $\overline{y}$ have a uniform relation between their respective equilibrium factor-intensities. In other words, we are abandoning our "pure" categories *S* and *Z*. Instead, it is assumed that factor reversals can occur any number of times.

As is well known, if factor reversals occur, then for some specific relative input prices *R* factor proportions will be the same in the two industries, and to one side of such input proportions one industry will be relatively intensively using the factor which it uses relatively less intensively to the other side of the specific input propor-portions. The relation between $\overline{R}$ and *R* thus is a "composite" one, in some ranges revealing the pattern of the *SS* function and in others that of the *ZZ* function in Figures 3-a and 3-b. In other words, the relation between relative input and output prices no longer is single-valued with respect to both axes, but rather reveals maxima and/or minima for $\overline{R}$.

We have shown one such simple relation, involving only one maximum, in Figure 11, leaving it to the reader to study for himself others involving multiple reversals and a minimum $\overline{R}$. One thing must be clear: the locus must remain single-valued with respect to the R-axis because, for a prescribed R, prices of both outputs in a competitive economy are uniquely given. A related property—one by far the most important—is that the absolute value of the elasticity of $\bar{R}$ with respect to R, as before (in the pure S and Z cases), must be less than unity on the assumptions we have made about the production functions. This property, proof of which is the same as that presented in Chapter IV, guarantees both uniqueness

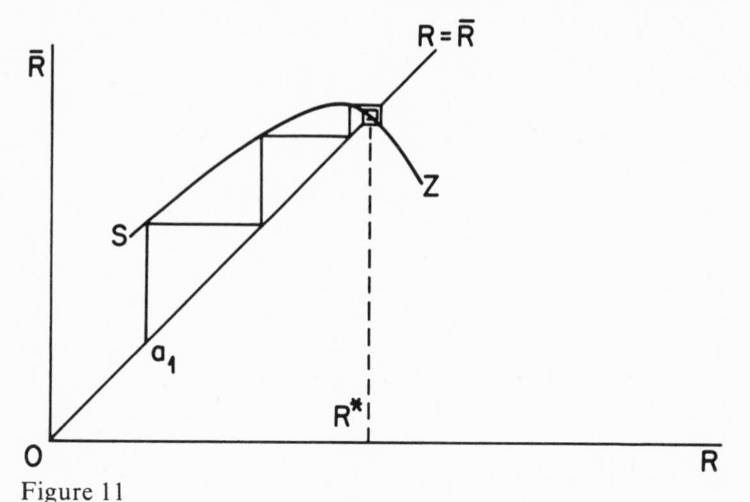

Figure 11

of $R^* = \bar{R}^*$ and convergence toward R^* from an initial $R \neq R^*$ as we travel along an intertemporally efficient path. The uniqueness of $R^* = \bar{R}^*$ together with the analysis in Chapter V guarantees a unique V^*. (Note that that analysis does not change at all, because with a unique R^* there can be only one set of factor proportions in each of the two industries, and thus, again, output proportions are the only variables of the analysis.) As is shown in Figure 11, however, $R^* = \bar{R}^*$ now may be approached first smoothly and then through a cobweb. Alternatively, as the reader may verify, the process can start with a cobweb and end up smoothly, or the two types of approach can change several times between the initial point and the point $R^* = \overline{R}^*$.

Correspondingly, an equilibrium path leading from T_1 to some T_N can proceed alternatingly in a smooth and zigzag manner, as shown in Figure 12. Significantly, nothing changes about the existence or validity of the turnpike theorem. It will be noted that the funnels $F(N)$ (such as that illustrated in Figure 12) still are defined, the

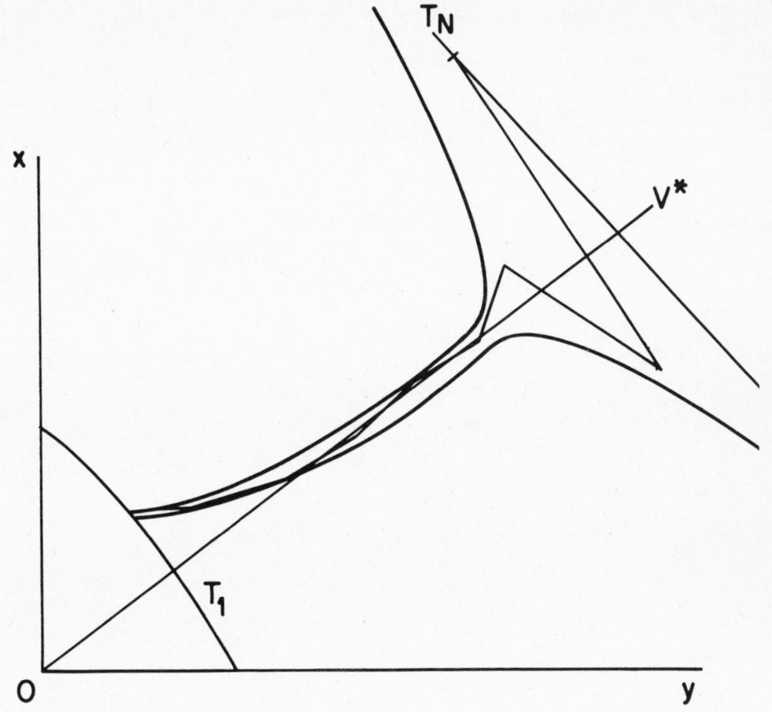

Figure 12

loci $f(-n)$ and $f'(-n)$ of Chapter VIII still must converge toward each other with increasing n, and T_N must tend towards linearity with increasing N; the only difference now is that the loci f will all be to one side of V in the situation of smooth ranges of the adjustment of R, and alternating with the loci f' in the situation when the adjustment in R proceeds through a cobweb.

XIII. The case of technological change

Thus far, like Von Neumann and most others writing on the present subject, we have made the assumption that the production functions are invariant with respect to time. In this chapter that assumption is relaxed. First it is shown that with appropriate general modifications most of what has been shown for the case of constant technology also pertains when technological change is of the Hicks-neutral variety in both industries, proceeding at the same rate in each period (not necessarily at the same rate among periods). Afterward, I will make a few conjectures about the far more difficult growth situations involving other types of technological progress.

Suppose that in period 0, technologies are the same as those assumed thus far. The locus T_1 in Figure 1 thus remains unaltered. In the next period, however, each process becomes g_1 per cent more efficient in the Hicks-neutral manner (that is, the isoquants shift by g_1 per cent in both industries). Each point on T_1 will thus lead to a new production possibility locus such as t_2 in Figure 1, but that locus will be "blown up" by g_1 per cent away from the origin in comparison with the locus (such as t_2) based on constant technologies. The new envelope T_2 will thus also be a homothetic g_1 per cent augmentation of the original (without technical change) contour T_2 as drawn in the diagram. Similarly, the new T_3 will be obtained from the old T_3-locus (without technical change) by applying to the old T_3 a homothetic augmentation factor $(1 + g_1)(1 + g_2) - 1$, where g_2 is the Hicks-neutral per cent technical progress in both industries in production period 2. In general, T_N is obtained from the original T_N by the application of an augmentation factor $(1 - g_1) \dots (1 - g_{N-1}) - 1$, the g_i's indicating the rate of Hicks-neutral technical change in period i.

Because the SS, ZZ, and SZ lines as defined and discussed in Chapters IV and XII are invariant with respect to technical progress of the Hicks-neutral variety and at the same rate in both industries, any efficient path in the new situation (with technical change) will be a "homothetic replica" of the old one (without technical change). Corresponding to the same T_1 and the same point on T_1, a point A_i of the new path will be on the same ray through the origin as the old one, but relatively $(1 + g_1) \dots (1 + g_{i-1}) - 1$ as far from the origin. In particular, since the new V^* is such a replica of the old V^*, the two rays V^* are identical, whatever the g_i; moreover, because our turnpike theorem involves only angular, and not absolute distances, and because all funnels with technical change are homothetic translations of corresponding funnels without technical change (note that the sides of the funnels are also efficient paths), the turnpike theorem must also hold. Actually, except for the "homothetic translation" just explained, all that has been shown in the preceding chapters pertains also to the case with Hicks-neutral technical progress, identical in both industries in each particular period.

About all other types of technical progress, very little more can be said than that the problem becomes exceedingly difficult. One conclusion—with obviously shifting functions relating R and $\bar{R}$—is that except for the sheerest of coincidences, there cannot be a V^* of the type discussed thus far. However—and this is a conjecture based on this writer's intuition more than on anything else—all points on any efficient frontier in the x-y plane still should be attainable through an appropriate efficient path, and the funnels of efficient paths, such as the $F(N)$ discussed above, corresponding to a horizon T_N should be becoming arbitrarily "slim" at a given time period $i_0(<N)$ for N sufficiently large.

XIV. The case of more than two products

Only a little reflection is necessary to realize that the extension of the foregoing to a situation of an arbitrary number of inputs and outputs is quite straightforward. Without trying to provide rigorous proofs, my purpose in this chapter is to assist the reader in performing for himself such a generalization. While attempting to stay as much as possible within the framework of an arbitrary number of inputs and outputs—the latter again being produced through single-product and continuous technologies—I will illustrate some of the key arguments through a three-product diagrammatic example. By symmetry with our preceding discussion, I will assume in the first part of this chapter that each product uses all inputs; this assumption will be relaxed later on, and some interesting results will be derived for the three-product case where one production process uses only two inputs.

Suppose first that there are *n* products, characterized as inputs by the vector $\mathbf{X}$ and as outputs by the vector $\bar{\mathbf{X}}$. The reader should have no difficulty in visualizing that given the smooth single-product technologies (as postulated above) and an initial endowment $\mathbf{X}_0$, there will be the usual concave production-possibility locus for period

1, T_1. Each point of T_1 can then constitute the productive resources for outputs in the second period, described by another concave production possibility, and the envelope of all such individual production loci, in turn, leads to T_2, as it did in the two-product situation. In a similar way, further frontiers T_i are derived from the next-inferior frontiers T_{i-1}. It is implicit in this construction that to a point A_i on T_i can correspond only one efficient point on T_{i+1} and only one efficient point on T_{i-1}, such points belonging to the efficient path A passing through A_i.

Turning to the Von Neumann path and the turnpike theorem, we first realize that to an efficient path A (including points A_1 through A_m) uniquely corresponds a path (a collection) of "equilibrium" relative input and output prices $\mathbf{R}_1 = \overline{\mathbf{R}}_1$ through $\mathbf{R}_m = \overline{\mathbf{R}}_m$, where each $\mathbf{R}$ is a vector of $n - 1$ elements. As in the two-product case, once a point A_1 on T_1 is selected, the equilibrium set of relative input and output prices $\mathbf{R}_1 = \overline{\mathbf{R}}_1$ is known (from the partial derivatives, or "slopes," of T_1). But under perfectly competitive conditions, A_1 and $\mathbf{R}_1$ are all that is needed to determine $\mathbf{R}_2 = \overline{\mathbf{R}}_2$ (of course, given the n technologies). With $\mathbf{R}_2$ known and A_2 also given (through the envelope construction described above), we get $\mathbf{R}_3 = \overline{\mathbf{R}}_3$, and so forth, for all subsequent $\mathbf{R}_i = \overline{\mathbf{R}}_i$ and A_i, as long as the efficient path A lasts (of course we know, for example, that for the path V asymptotic to V^* the lasting or "duration" of the path is infinite).

The simple accounting step leading from $\mathbf{R}_i$ to $\overline{\mathbf{R}}_{i+1}$ is embodied in a set of n equations in which the necessary $n \times n$ unit input coefficients are uniquely determined for a prescribed $\mathbf{R}_i$. Postulating equality of $\mathbf{R}_i$ and $\overline{\mathbf{R}}_{i+1}$, as we did for the two-product situation in Chapter V, the n equations lead to $\mathbf{R}^* = \overline{\mathbf{R}}^*$. For the moment we have only to postulate the existence of $\mathbf{R}^* = \overline{\mathbf{R}}^*$; the uniqueness of that solution will be shown later.

To $\mathbf{R}^*$, given the technologies assumed, corresponds a unique set of $n \times n$ unit input coefficients, and—as in our construction in Figure 4 for the two-product case—to these input coefficients uniquely corresponds a set of total "national" inputs $\mathbf{X}_i^*$ and outputs $\overline{\mathbf{X}}_{i+1}^*$ which are proportional, that is, $\overline{\mathbf{X}}_{i+1}^* = c\mathbf{X}_i^*$, where c is a constant scalar. A set of such inputs and outputs then defines the linear Von Neumann path V^* (passing through the origin) associated with $\mathbf{R}^*$. There will be as many V^*'s as there are solutions $\mathbf{R}^*$. Of course, we know that there will be only one V^* and one $\mathbf{R}^*$—but this is something yet to be shown. For this, and for the general discussion of the funnels and the turnpike theorem, we must turn to Figure 13.

On T_i shown in that diagram in an x-y-z space we find a contour marked $f_i(-1)$. It is the intersection of T_i with the (now three-dimensional and thus more realistic) funnel $F(i + 1)$. Alternatively, $f_i(-1)$ should be understood as the intersection of T_i with $f(-1)$, a conelike locus of points analogous to $f(-1)$ and $f'(-1)$ from the two-product situation. As required, $f_i(-1)$ passes through points a, b, and c, which are points of tangency between the highest attainable isoquants of the three production functions and T_i. As indicated for points a and b, efficient paths passing through these points terminate at a' and b' on the x and y axes respectively; a' and b' are intercepts of T_{i+1} with the two coordinate axes. The whole contour $f_i(-1)$ is obtained by a method similar to that used in the two-product case. For example, the segment stretching between a and b is generated as a locus of the points of tangency between T_i and Scitovsky-type indifference surfaces, each belonging to a homogeneous family of surfaces uniquely defined by a point on the broken locus a'-b', that is, defined by given proportions of outputs of x and y, with zero output of z.

The contour on T_i inside $f_i(-1)$—not marked—is nothing but $f_i(-2)$ belonging to $f(-2)$ and to $F(i+2)$, and similarly, *mutatis mutandis*, for the contour within $f_i(-2)$, which is $f_i(-3)$; and so forth, ad infinitum, that is, through to the contour $f_i(-\infty)$. The latter is only a single point, coinciding with $F(\infty)$ at T_i and with V, the path asymptotic to V^*. The loci f_i cannot intersect each other or themselves (for example, to form something like a figure eight). These conclusions follow from the conditions

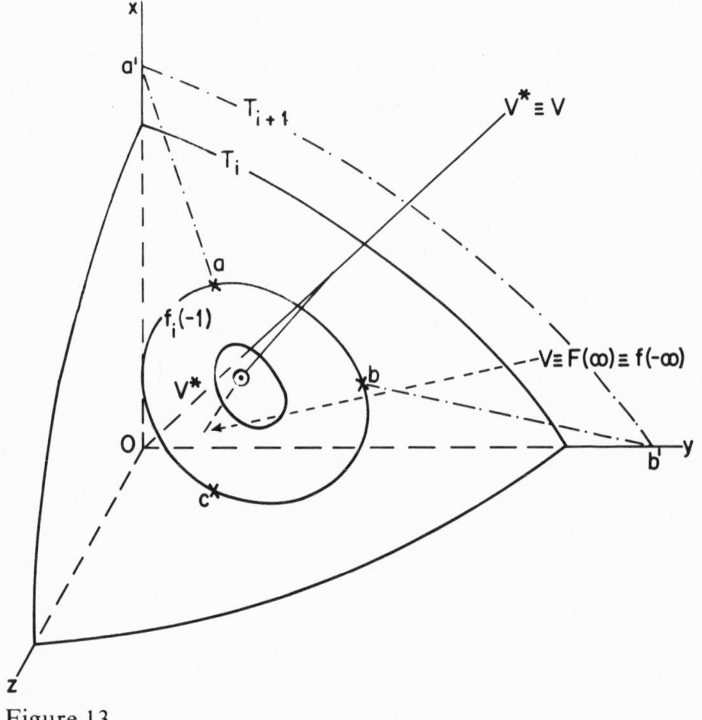

Figure 13

of nonintersection of efficient paths (that is, the impossibility of two paths passing through one point); note that if such an intersection of two f's took place, two different paths would also intersect at the intersection point, each belonging to the side (wall) of another funnel. On the other hand, a "self-intersection" of a single f_i is impossible, because such an occurrence would again imply the intersection of efficient paths, and this contradicts what we know about these paths.

Leaving it to the reader to establish for himself that a contour $f_i(-j)$ can never be on the outside of $f_i(-j + 1)$, we can conclude from that fact and from what has been said thus far that there can be only one point on each T_i representing V, $F(\infty)$, and $f(-\infty)$; and thus the situation depicted in Figure 13 is a necessary one. Recalling that V is the path asymptotic to V^*, from the uniqueness of V we conclude that there can be only one V^*; but from what has been said above about the relation between V^* and $R^* = \bar{R}^*$, we conclude that there can be only one $R^* = \bar{R}^*$.

Because V is asymptotic to V^*, we know that the angular distance between the two loci measured along T_i can be made arbitrarily small for i sufficiently large. Moreover, we know that the "ring" $f_i(-j)$ can be made arbitrarily small for a given i provided that j is large enough. The two facts combined lead to the conclusion that a funnel $F(N)$ can be made an arbitrary fraction of times nearer to V^* than a prescribed small angle e, for N sufficiently large. Suppose that in a specific instance such a number N is N_0. A funnel $F(N_0 + k)$ (with k a positive integer) cannot be further away than e from V^* than is $F(N_0)$—with e small and N_0 large—because for periods N_0 and higher, the T_i's again, as in the two-product situation, become infinitesimally near to being linear and parallel to each other. This turns the loci $f(-j)$ into conic surfaces generated by straight lines all passing through the origin, a condition which, as we have seen, is sufficient to complete the proof of the turnpike theorem, as formulated in Chapter X. While we have been referring a good deal to the three-product case in our exposition—especially in the latter part of our discussion—it should be clear to the reader that what has been said is also valid for the n-product situation.

The analytical apparatus of the present chapter lends itself well to showing the consequences of a growth situation (thus far ruled out by assumption) where a technology does not use one (or, by implication, more) of the products as an input. The results are not markedly different from those obtained thus far. The only new thing, in a case where $\bar{x}$ is produced from, say, x and y only, is that a point such as a in Figure 13 now will be at the intercept of T_i with the x-y plane, and the locus $f_i(-1)$ will thus be tangential to the x-y plane at that point. More generally, the whole locus $f(-1)$ will be touching the x-y plane along a line generated by the tangencies of the two-dimensional isoquants of x in the x-y plane and the intercepts of the T_i's with that plane. All the rest of the analysis in this chapter remains basically unaltered. In a very broad and superficial sense it can be said that together with $f(-1)$ all the other surfaces f and all the funnels will be pulled, so to speak, towards the x-y plane, and thus the absence of z from the technology of x can be said to render all the conceivable turnpikes less z-intensive than they would have been otherwise.

XV. The case of fixed coefficients

It is only at this stage of our argument that we come to what may be termed the more conventional or traditional setting of Von Neumann's growth situation; namely, the setting of activities defined by fixed coefficients.[17] Of course, we are retaining for the time being our assumption of no joint products. Thus, what we will be concerned with in this chapter is a situation where the two outputs $\bar{x}$ and $\bar{y}$ are produced through Leontief-type technologies:

$$\bar{x} = \min(x/a_{xx}; y/a_{yx}) \qquad (1')$$

and

$$\bar{y} = \min(x/a_{xy}; y/a_{yy}) \qquad (2')$$

where the four a's are the well-known fixed input-output coefficients, the first subscript indicating the nature of the input (the supplying industry) and the second subscript indicating the using industry.

Before we turn to the details of our analysis, a few general words of introduction are called for. In fact, the situation we are about to examine is a special case of the

[17]The analysis of the present chapter partly overlaps that of Hicks's "Prices and the Turnpike I: The Story of a Mare's Nest," *Review of Economic Studies,* XXVIII (1961), 77–88.

more general "continuous" (or neoclassical) situation that we have studied before. However, the presence of discontinuities which obviously are implied by the technologies (1′) and (2′) makes the transition from the general to the special case somewhat less than obvious in several respects. Consequently, it is useful to spell out the various stages of the analysis—as known to us from the foregoing chapters—in some detail. Second, it is clearly desirable to translate as far as possible the present analysis into the conventional framework of fixed coefficients. Finally, probably the most important reason for undertaking the present analysis is that the fixed-coefficient case is actually a completely linear case containing (in a manner similar to that known to us already from the identical-technology situation) in a certain sense the very essence of the general case; propositions which are only approximately true in the continuous case, or which, to be true, require a large number of periods, turn out to be exact descriptions, for any time horizon, of the "Leontief world" to be examined here. But all this will become more apparent as we proceed with our analysis. In what follows we restrict ourselves to the S-case, leaving the more or less obvious extensions concerning the Z-case to the reader.

Probably the least different from what is to us already familiar is the variation of relative prices associated with a movement along an efficient path (the exact meaning of "efficient" will be explained presently). Whether with or without fixed coefficients, under competitive conditions a relative product price $\bar{R}$ uniquely corresponds to a prescribed relative input price R (recall that we have defined R as p_y/p_x). With fixed coefficients, as shown in Figure 14, we actually know that the SS locus—analogous to that in Figure 3-a—must vary between a lower limit $\bar{R}_1' = a_{xy}/a_{xx}$ and an upper limit $\bar{R}_1 = a_{yy}/a_{yx}$ (recall that in the *S*-case here considered, $\bar{x}$ is relatively *x*-intensive and $\bar{y}$ is *y*-intensive). More exactly, $\bar{R}$ varies with R according to a segment of a hyperbola—the segment corresponding to $R \geq 0$—of the form

$$\bar{R} = \frac{a_{yy}R + a_{xy}}{a_{yx}R + a_{xx}} \qquad (5)$$

The reader will have no difficulty in realizing that the numerator and denominator of the fraction in (5) are nothing but the unit cost of $\bar{y}$ and $\bar{x}$ respectively, both divided by p_x. In the context of the variation of R and $\bar{R}$ along an efficient path, as will be recalled from our discussion in Chapter IV, the date of R precedes by one period that of $\bar{R}$; it is this time lag that leads to our familiar price-adjustment cobweb (we will return to it presently when we discuss the efficient growth paths). The reader also may find it useful to verify on the basis of relation (5) that the elasticity of $\bar{R}$ with respect to R must be less than unity—a conclusion already obtained for the

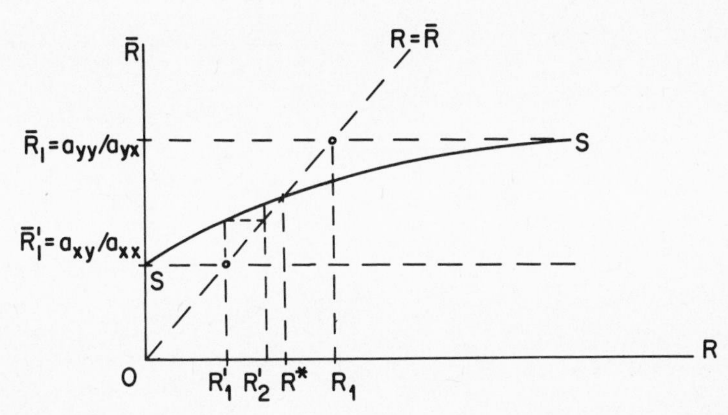

Figure 14

general case in Chapter IV. Moreover, it is now easy to obtain R^* and $\bar{R}^*$ by substituting R for $\bar{R}$ in (5) and solving the resulting quadratic equation. We observe from Figure 14 that there can be only one positive and real root; consequently R^* must be the larger of the two roots, namely

$$R^* = \bar{R}^* = \frac{a_{yy} - a_{xx} + \left| \sqrt{a_{yy} - a_{xx})^2 + 4a_{yx}a_{xy}} \right|}{2a_{yx}} \tag{6}$$

More could be said about the variation in R, but it will be preferable to do so in conjunction with the analysis of efficient paths, to which we now turn. In Figure 15 the data of a typical situation are given by the initial endowment L_0, the two rays marked (x) and (y) reflecting the ratios of input coefficients of the two technologies, and the postulate that point b in the box diagram formed by the initial endowments L_0 reflects one unit of output of each product.

As before, the maximum attainable outputs in the first

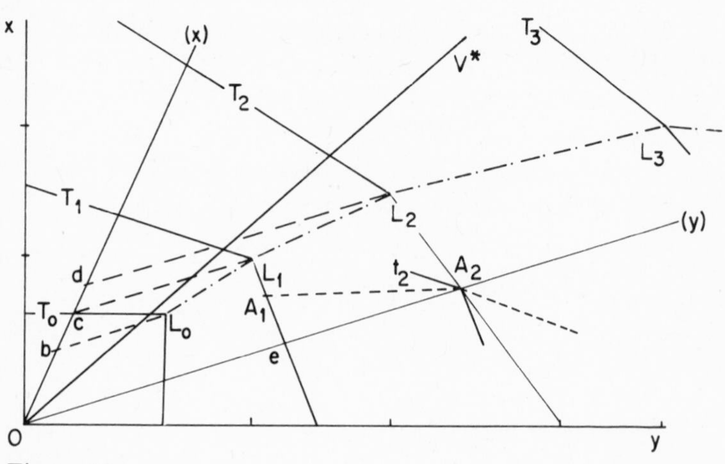

Figure 15

period are given by T_1, and efficient points attainable in period 2, T_2, are obtained as an envelope of production-possibility loci corresponding to individual points of T_1. For example, A_1 on T_1 determines uniquely the production possibility t_2 enveloped at A_2 by T_2. Noting that the two slopes found on t_2 must be the same as those found on T_1 (that is, $\bar{R}_1'$ and $\bar{R}_1$ respectively) and noting from Figure 14 that in period 2, $\bar{y}$ must be relatively cheaper than in period 1 (that is, $R_2 < \bar{R}_1$ or T_2 is flatter than T_1 below the vertex), we realize that the enveloping must take place at the vertex of t_2—and similarly for all production possibilities such as t_2 corresponding to all points on T_1 such as A_1. This result leads to the two conclusions that all points on T_2 must be points generated by full employment of resources (recall that the vertices such as A_2 are the only full-employment points of loci such as t_2) and that there is a unique correspondence between points on T_1 and T_2, the two points being connected by an efficient path.

Similarly, T_3 is generated as an envelope of vertices of individual production-possibility loci, each stemming from a point on T_2. Consequently, the one-to-one correspondence just noted also exists between points of T_2 and T_3, and all outputs on T_3 involve full employment of resources in period 2. The two slopes of T_3 are given by the cobweb of Figure 14. Realizing that the derivation of T_4, T_5, and the rest is always analogous, we can thus conclude that once a point on T_1 is picked, all the future points of the corresponding efficient path connecting the efficient envelopes T_i are determined. Moreover, we know that for all efficient paths originating south of L_1, equilibrium R_i's and $\bar{R}_i'$s will be the same, as they will for paths originating north of L_1 (this conclusion is different from the neoclassical case where the initial R_1 is a continuous variable).

The vertices of the envelopes T_i such as the points L_i in Figure 15 are simply obtained as output points corresponding to inputs given by L_{i-1}. To the relative prices along L—which at first sight appear indeterminate—we will return below. Including the L-path just noted, three possible patterns are to be distinguished for any efficient path (any path connecting the efficient frontiers T_i): paths passing through T_1 (1) north of, (2) at, and (3) south of the Von Neumann path V^*. (V^* is determined exactly in the same way as in Chapter V, the key input coefficients underlying that determination now being the unique coefficients a_{xx}, a_{xy}, a_{yx}, and a_{yy} rather than the specific coefficients of the neoclassical situation corresponding to R^* and $\bar{R}^*$.) Paths of type (1) will continuously be "drifting" (deflecting) upward, away from V^*; paths of type (2) will remain indefinitely with V^*; and those of type (3), such as the path L in Figure 15, will be drifting downward, also away from V^*. These conclusions should be quite evident to the reader from our discussion in Chapter V; they will also be reascertained for the specific case of fixed coefficients in the following chapter, where we deal with efficient funnels and the turnpike theorem.

At this stage of the argument I would like to make a few general remarks by way of summary of what has been shown thus far in this chapter. Given prescribed (Leontief-type) technologies and starting from given initial endowments (such as L_0 in the diagram), an intertemporally efficient economy, whatever its future target, will experience full employment in all except period 0. Its relative prices will indefinitely be approaching R^*—as given by relation (6)—and thus the slopes of the two linear segments below and above the only possible discontinuity of T_i will be becoming more alike, and the discontinuity (such as points L_i in Figure 15) will gradually be drifting out of (or to the confines of) the first quadrant except in the special situation where the initial endowments coincide with V^*. Thus, except for that special case, the entire T_i will turn into a straight line for a finite period i, and the slope of T_i then will be approaching R^* with increasing i. Whether that approach of R^* will be from below or from above will depend—as is apparent from the construction of Figure 15—on whether V^* intersects T_1 in the range whose absolute slope is R_1 or in the range corresponding to R_1'.

I have postponed answering the question of what relative prices of $\bar{x}$ and $\bar{y}$—if any—correspond to a path such as the path of the L_i's in Figure 15, or any other part of vertexes of the T_i's. It seems to me that the answer is not entirely unambiguous. The relative prices are indeterminate in the sense that at a point such as L_1 there is no technical marginal rate of transformation of x into y such as there is for all other points of T_1. If initial prices are specified for period 1 not exceeding the range R_1 through R_1', however, then in a fully competitive economy all subsequent price ratios are determinate through the SS relation in Figure 14. While relative prices may be indeterminate at the vertex for a finite time period, they are determinate for T_∞ at the level R^*, because the corner of the vertex disappears, the two "arms" of T then forming a single line.

Finally, and probably most important, the question can be answered in the context of a linear-programing problem, as is done by Dorfman, Samuelson, and Solow.[18] Since we will examine the work of these three

[18] *Op. cit.*

authors in Chapter XVII, we can postpone a more careful discussion of this subject until then. At present, let it only be observed that in the case of a programing problem, what we really are doing is to specify prices for a terminal period N, and if such prices are consistent with the vertex solution in the terminal period (that is, with L_N on T_N; see Figure 15), all the price ratios for periods preceding N are then determined (backward) from the terminal price ratio through relation (5), or through a construction of the type shown in Figure 14 (of course, now moving in the direction away from R^*).

XVI. Efficient funnels and the turnpike theorem in the case of fixed coefficients

The special case of fixed coefficients is perhaps most revealing in the context of the turnpike theorem and the study of efficient-path funnels (as introduced in Chapter VIII). Not only can the turnpike theorem be stated with somewhat greater generality than in Chapter IX, but its proof becomes so simple that some may find it bordering on triviality.

The simplicity of the fixed-coefficients situation and the corresponding conclusions sought will become apparent to the reader well before we are through with the analysis of the present chapter, once he realizes that the loci f and f' introduced and explained in Chapter VIII must now be straight lines coincident (in the region to the right and above T_1) with rays through the origin.[19] For f's corresponding to 1, 2, 3, 4, and ∞, such a pattern is illustrated in Figure 16 together with the Von Neumann ray V^*, two efficient frontiers T_1 and T_4, and initial conditions A_0. Recalling that $f(-1)$ and $f'(-1)$ are nothing but loci of

[19] It will be recalled that the loci $f(-n)$ and $f'(-n)$ are loci connecting intersections of the efficient frontiers T_i with funnel-boundaries of funnels terminating in n periods—i.e., of funnels $f(i + n)$.

tangency between the two isoquant maps—(characterized by (x) and (y) in the diagram)—and the efficient frontiers T_i (for all $i > 0$), the linearity of $f(-1)$ and $f'(-1)$ and the fact that these loci must coincide with rays through the origin immediately follow from the constancy of input coefficients of the two technologies, and the negative slopes of $T_i (i > 0)$—recall that the latter property was established in the preceding chapter.

Consider now $f(-1)$. It clearly corresponds to a constant ratio of outputs—call the ratio $(\bar{x}/\bar{y})_1$. As we have seen in Chapter VII, to $(\bar{x}/\bar{y})_1$ uniquely corresponds a family of homogeneous isoquants of the Scitovsky variety

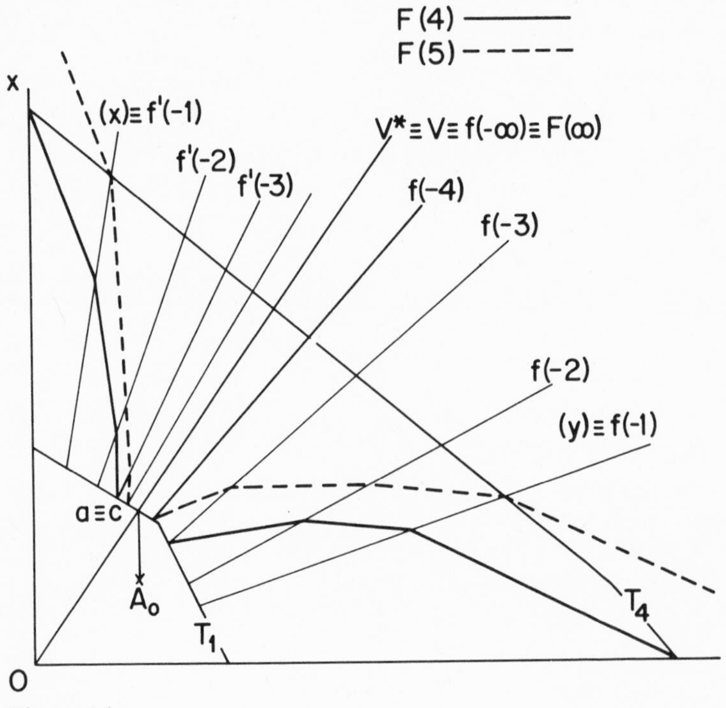

Figure 16

(also familiar to us from Chapter VII). By Conclusion IV of that chapter, that family must be relatively more x-intensive than the isoquant map of product $\bar{y}$—characterized by (y) in the diagram—because the latter map is actually a Scitovsky map corresponding to $(\bar{x}/\bar{y})_0 = 0$ (that is, to the proportions along the y-axis) and thus $(\bar{x}/\bar{y})_1 > (\bar{x}/\bar{y})_0$. As is well known, a Scitovsky map derived from two Leontief-type isoquant maps for a constant $\bar{x}/\bar{y}$ is itself a homogeneous and right-angled Leontief-type map.[20] But this being so, $f(-2)$, which is the locus of tangencies of the Scitovsky-map corresponding to $(\bar{x}/\bar{y})_1$ with the T_i frontiers, cannot be anything else but a straight line characterized by a constant $\bar{x}/\bar{y}$ ratio; call that ratio $(\bar{x}/\bar{y})_2$. Because $(\bar{x}/\bar{y})_1 > (\bar{x}/\bar{y})_0$; by Conclusion IV of Chapter VII we know that $(\bar{x}/\bar{y})_2 > (\bar{x}/\bar{y})_1$. Along similar lines we find that $f(-3)$ must be straight, aiming at the origin, and above $f(-2)$; and in general, using the reasoning we have just gone through, any two loci $f(-j)$ and $f'(-j)$ must coincide with straight lines passing through the origin and must be enclosed by $f(-j + 1)$ and $f'(-j + 1)$.

We know already from our earlier discussion of the general case that the process of convergence of the f and f' loci has a limit, the path V, coinciding with the Von Neumann path V^*, at an infinite time horizon. But it follows from the divergence of all efficient paths other than V^* from V^* that the only path coinciding with V

[20]If the proposition is not known to the reader he can easily verify it by sliding back to back two Leontief isoquants for prescribed constant levels of $\bar{x}^0$ and $\bar{y}^0$ and tracing a contour by placing the pencil at the origin of the sliding isoquant. The result is a Scitovsky-Leontief isoquant, characteristic of a homogeneous map corresponding to $\bar{x}^0/\bar{y}^0$

at T_∞ is V^* itself, and thus $V = V^*$. Consequently, at any T_i with a finite i, $V^* = f(-\infty) = f'(-\infty)$,[21] and $F(\infty)$, the funnel of efficient paths leading to the frontier in infinity, must also coincide with V^* at any T_i with a finite i. From these conclusions it further follows—contrary to the neoclassical case—that with fixed coefficients any $F(N)$ must contain V^* at all T_i, for $1 \leq i \leq N$ and in particular at T_1. Moreover, from the constancy of x/y proportions at any given f or f' locus and the fact that higher-indexed f-lines are enclosed by the lower-indexed ones, it follows that the angular (and in fact the absolute) distance between V^* and the boundaries of a given F (measured along the T_i's) must be uniformly increasing as we move from T_1 to T_2, T_3, and so on.

The simplicity of the turnpike theorem pointed out earlier should now also be quite apparent. Consider the funnel $F(4)$ (originating at T_1 and terminating at T_4) containing all the efficient paths leading from A_0 to all points of T_4 *between the frontiers T_1 and T_4*. The bottom of the funnel—that is, the range of T_1 between $f(-3)$ and $f'(-3)$—corresponds to an angular distance e of about $e_0 = 25°$. Consequently, the funnel or any of its paths cannot be further from V^* than e_0, measured angularly along any T_i, more than three times. Now suppose that the time horizon is expanded from 4 to 5 and we consider $F(5)$. The linearity of the f loci and the fact that $F(4)$

[21] A careful reader may ask the question: How do we know that the process of derivation of the loci f and f' converges "all the way" to V^*, reached for $f(\infty)$ and $f'(\infty)$. The answer is as follows: We know it because if it were not so, a "vacuum" (devoid of any efficient paths) would have to exist on either side of V^*; but this is impossible because we know (from the analysis of the preceding section) that, for example, every point of T_1 in the vicinity of V^* is a point of an efficient path.

encloses $F(5)$ immediately tells us that the maximum number of times $F(5)$ (or any path within it) can be further from V^* than e_0 again is three. And similarly, we know that any $F(N)$, with $N > 3$, cannot be further than e_0 from V^* more than three times.

As in the neoclassical case, the linearity of the loci f and f', and the fact that they correspond to constant output-proportions, is the important ingredient of the proof of the turnpike theorem. But in the Leontief-type situation considered here, that linearity is present for all time horizons and consequently the theorem holds "exactly" for any specified distance e between 0 and 90 degrees. In the neoclassical case a *small* angular distance e had to be postulated in order to push the horizon N_m^e (see the statement of the theorem in Chapter IX) far enough into the future to render the loci f and f' infinitesimally near linearity and constancy of x/y proportions.[22]

An observation related to the remarks just made is that in the fixed-coefficients situation with which we are dealing here, not only the Von Neumann ray (for which it is true always) but also all the loci f and f' are independent of the initial conditions and thus of the specific forms and positions of the efficient frontiers T_i. And thus, for example, the turnpike case discussed above, corresponding to the specified distance $e_0 = 25°$, must pertain to a growth situation defined by the specific technologies and

[22]Of course, if we are willing to add, in the neoclassical case, a few periods—so to speak "for good measure"—to the minimum number of periods when a funnel is further than e from V^*, even the neoclassical case then can have its turnpike theorem valid for $F(N)$ with a small N. For example, we can be quite sure that in the neoclassical case whose f and f' lines coincide with those of Figure 16 for large N no more than 4 (rather than 3) periods can have funnels further than e from V^*, for any N, large or small; and if 4 is not the number, then 5 certainly is.

any initial capital stocks (A_0). Specifically, the maximum number *three* of those periods when any F can be further away from V^* than e_0 pertains to all F, whatever the initial endowments.

Another observation, implicit in most of this chapter and the last, but not yet stated quite explicitly, is that—again contrary to the neoclassical case—with Leontief-type technologies a point on an efficient path, say, the jth, is uniquely determined by the position of the $j - 1$st point and not—as in the neoclassical case—by the position *and* the marginal rate of transformation at the $j - 1$st point. This conclusion immediately follows from the fact, established in the preceding chapter, that except for production period 0 all efficient-path points are full-employment points, and from the fact that the technologies are of the fixed-coefficient and single-output (or Leontief) variety.

More will be said along these lines in the next chapter where we comment on Dorfman, Samuelson, and Solow's analysis of a case very similar to that studied here. Only one slight generalization remains to be discussed at present: There is no reason why each of the two products should be producible by a single production process; many efficient processes can exist, each corresponding to a different set of factor prices. Of course, in this context the neoclassical situation to which most of this study is devoted, corresponding to a continuum of techniques depending on a continuum of an infinite number of conceivable factor-price ratios, is a limiting case.

The reader may find it enjoyable to verify through a box-diagram construction that with more than one process for each product the first-period frontier T_1 may have more than one vertex; of course, it remains nonconvex.

And similarly, the subsequent higher T_i's may also have more than one corner. For i very large, however, even a single corner becomes extremely unlikely, and for $i = \infty$ such an occurrence is impossible. Further, it can be shown that as in the single-technology case there must always be full employment along all efficient paths except for production period 0; that is, the initial endowments may not be fully employed. The common sense of this proposition is, as before, that the T_i's are envelopes of some underlying t_i's (transformation loci corresponding to a single point in period $i - 1$) and that the enveloping cannot take place at a point other than a vertex of the t_i which always must be a point generated by full employment of resources.

XVII. Critical notes on the analysis by Dorfman, Samuelson, and Solow

In chapter 12 of their study on linear programing, Dorfman, Samuelson, and Solow analyze, among other things, efficient programs of capital accumulation on the assumption of Leontief-type (fixed coefficient) technologies.[23] Except for the fact that their model of capital accumulation permits of nonzero consumption, its characteristics are basically the same as those defining the situation studied in the foregoing two chapters. Consequently, our work can throw some additional light on their conclusions. While more will be said below about the similarity of approaches, let it be noted here regarding our assumption of no consumption that it does not affect the results in a significant manner and, moreover, that it will be relaxed in Chapter XVIII.

As we did in our analysis in the preceding two chapters, Dorfman, Samuelson, and Solow consider a situation of two single-product activities producing $\bar{x}$ and $\bar{y}$ respectively (they call them S_1 and S_2) in period $i + 1$ from inputs of x and y in period i, the inputs being related to outputs through prescribed fixed coefficients. The three

[23] Dorfman, Samuelson, and Solow, *op. cit.*

authors prefer to think of their two capitals S_1 and S_2 as stocks available in a given period from which consumption and additions to stocks are produced in the next period. But because the only restriction they impose on S_1 and S_2 is that these magnitudes should never become negative (that is, all points of a production possibility frontier in the first quadrant are permissible), the technical characteristics of their model with zero consumption are exactly the same as those implicit in the preceding two chapters. It is only a matter of interpretation, and not of substance, that we think of our model as one involving complete transformation of stocks, where Dorfman, Samuelson, and Solow think of a model as one involving production, by means of given stocks, of (positive or negative) net additions to these stocks.

With these remarks and the analysis of the preceding two chapters in mind, we can now turn to the results obtained, or the conjectures stated, by Dorfman, Samuelson, and Solow. The first to be noted is the result regarding the shape of the efficient attainable frontiers T_i: the three authors expect them to assume the form of "an angular polygon or polyhedron, with flat faces and occasional sharp vertexes, or corners," as is also indicated in their Figure 12-11.[24] As we have shown in Chapter XV, on the assumptions made, there can be at most one vertex on any T_i, and, with i increasing to a large number (that is, in the very long run), excepting the case where the vertex on T_1 coincides with V^*, we can be virtually certain that T_i will turn into a straight line; it may also be useful to recall that for a large i these straight lines will be just about parallel, and their common slope will approximate the Von Neumann price ratio R^*.

[24] *Ibid.*, chap. 12.

From these conclusions it further follows that the linear programs considered by Dorfman, Samuelson, and Solow, designed to maximize the value of capital stock over a multiperiod horizon, will generally (though not absolutely necessarily) lead to intercept solutions, or what we may call fully unbalanced solutions, if long-range situations are envisaged. However, the prices (weights) of the objective function (called the K_j's by the three authors), will then provide us with the prices (the R's) for all the preterminal periods. Although neither their analysis nor ours is concerned with situations of more than two products, some of the extensions to a larger number of products are quite straightforward. In a three-product case, for example, T_i can have at most one vertex point and three ridge lines meeting at such a point, and except when V^* in period one coincides with the vertex or a ridge line, the whole T_i must turn sooner or later into a plane, and all planes then for a high i will be just about parallel.

In another place (section 12.3.4) the three authors define as *Leontief trajectories* all paths involving full employment of resources (capital) at all times (in particular also in period 0). They conjecture it to be a theorem— "not an easy one"— that all Leontief trajectories are efficient, that is, lead from one frontier T_i to the next T_{i+1}. We see from our analysis in Chapter XV that this must be so: in Figure 15 the only Leontief path is L_0, L_1, L_2, L_3, . . . (note that it is constructed exactly from the data inherent in the graph); it must be efficient because all points of T_{i+1}, as we have seen, represent outputs derived from full employment of inputs along T_i between the fixed-proportion lines marked (x) and (y), and because point L_i is among such points (on T_i).

The three authors continue by arguing that "the Leontief trajectory is one among an infinity of efficient paths, and each of the other efficient paths allows some excess capacity at one time or another."[25] This statement is true, but it falls far short of saying all that can be said. We have seen in Chapter XV that the "one time or another" really can be only period 0; thereafter, all the other efficient paths (besides the Leontief paths L_0, $L_1, \ldots$, in Figure 15), on the assumptions made, must also involve full employment at all times. To state the conclusion in a different and perhaps clearer way, if we take the whole locus T_1 (in Figure 15) as our initial condition—an approach that many might prefer—then all efficient paths in a given growth situation, whatever the time horizon, must also be Leontief paths.

Of course, it cannot be overemphasized that all these results are contingent on the assumptions made by the three authors and by us. If, for example, the additional constraint is imposed that a capital stock can never decline (this assumption is suggested in a footnote by Dorfman, Samuelson, and Solow) or that it can decline only by a prescribed maximum amount, the conclusion will have to be altered.

Implicit in all that has been done here and in the two previous chapters is that there may often be much simpler ways of solving a multiperiod linear program than the customary procedures of simplex or others. With full employment everywhere after period 0, the basic relations defining prices shown here (see Figure 14, for example) establish the link between the prices in the objective function and the interim prices; comparison between the terminal (objective-function) prices and the prices that

[25] *Ibid.*, p. 341.

would be obtained starting alternatively from $\overline{R}_1$ or $\overline{R}'_1$, after the prescribed number of time periods n (given as one of the data of the linear-programing problem), will indicate what type of specialization would occur or whether a vertex-solution could be involved in the terminal period.

With specialization definitely established in, say, $\overline{x}$ and recalling that full employment is involved throughout except for period 0, one can work backward, so to speak, from an arbitrary point on the x-axis along one side of a funnel for the prescribed number of periods minus one (that is, $n - 1$). Each step of this procedure involves finding full-employment inputs corresponding to prescribed outputs, the first such output point being on the x-axis. After $n - 1$ periods, except for scale, one finds oneself at a point on T_1. The true T_1 being easily obtainable from the technological data of the problem and the initial endowment, the scales then can be adjusted and all the physical solutions found. The shadow prices, on the other hand, are available from the computation (based on Figure 14) used to identify the nature of the solution. A similar, and even simpler, set of solutions can be obtained for the case where the terminal x/y ratio, rather than the terminal set of prices, is given.

If the comparison of the computed R's with the prices appearing in the objective function leads to the conclusion that there could be a vertex solution, there is nothing easier than to compute points of the Leontief path corresponding to the initial endowments and the prescribed technologies (a path such as L_0, L_1, $L_2, \ldots$) for the prescribed n periods, and see whether it falls within the first quadrant or not. If it does, we have the solution already; in the opposite situation, the procedure described above

—starting from one of the axes and working backward—is applicable.

As the reader may verify for himself, the fact that except for period 0 we must always have full employment, together with other results obtained here, can simplify the solution of the multiperiod linear-programing problem at hand in situations involving more than two products. Of course, the situation now becomes more complicated, whether we use the conventional method of solution or the one suggested here; but the latter still can have a significant comparative advantage.

XVIII. The case of long-range growth with nonzero consumption outlined

Until now we have discussed what many would term a strangely absurd world of Von Neumann's, where all outputs are at all times used as imputs and nothing is ever used for consumption, except, of course, insofar as humans are conceived of as machines with prescribed minimum food intakes (but the latter "humanization" may be more inhuman than a world of nothing but machines). If we have discussed extensively such a world, it was in part for expositional reasons, but primarily because, as far as I know, all the literature on the Von Neumann growth situation—including Von Neumann's initial contribution—and that dealing with generalizations of the turnpike variety never treat of states involving production for consumption. Dorfman, Samuelson, and Solow conceive of a world with prescribed zero or positive consumption levels for different periods when they study and derive the conditions of intertemporal efficiency (conditions which are identical with or without consumption). However, at the point where they come to the consideration of growth in the long run, and where they first enunciate the turnpike theorem, they revert to the world of no consumption.

The purpose of this chapter and the next is to recast the foregoing analysis in its major aspects, relaxing the assumption of zero consumption. Because the various categories, concepts, and analytical tools are familiar by now to the reader from the preceding chapters, while a good deal of the substance of the present analysis is comparatively novel, I propose to alter somewhat the procedure for these two chapters. In this chapter I will state and discuss the main conclusions of the case at hand in general terms so as to preserve the view of the whole and not have it obstructed by technical details or tedious proofs. In Chapter XIX I will turn to the more rigorous aspects of the matter.

The fundamental characteristics of efficient long-range growth with zero consumption—as we have already learned—are expressed in two distinct properties of the efficient funnels. The first is that an efficient funnel (the collection of all efficient paths corresponding to a given time horizon) will become arbitrarily slim at a given efficient frontier T_i for a sufficiently distant time-horizon defining the funnel. The second—more directly related to the turnpike theorem—is that *most* of the slim portion of the funnel will be very near to, or coincide with, the Von Neumann ray V^* (for the exact meaning of the terms "most" and "very" in this sentence, turn to Chapters IX and X). It will be recalled that an important locus related to both these properties is the path V, asymptotic to V^* and identical at any finite T_1 with both the funnel corresponding to an infinite time horizon $F(\infty)$ and the limiting loci $f(-\infty)$ and $f'(-\infty)$.

If the assumption of zero consumption is relaxed, the first property—of arbitrary slimness—remains and even is strengthened, as a general rule, in the sense that at T_n, a prescribed number of periods preceding the terminal horizon, an efficient funnel F_n will be thinner, measured angularly, with positive amounts of consumption than it would be with zero amounts. The second property, on the other hand, generally disappears (in a sense spelled out more precisely below). It can thus be said, perhaps more descriptively, that the path V, understood as a limit for the efficient funnels F and loci f and f', has its analogue in the nonzero consumption case, while the attribute of V being an asymptote to V^* generally is not preserved.

The Von Neumann path V^*, however, still has an important role to play in determining the position of V or —what is almost the same thing—the position of the slim portion of a long-range funnel. Some of the specifics underlying this statement will be shown rigorously in the next chapter. Here let me only summarize a few of the most important findings.

First, let it be noted that with a prescribed and erratic consumption pattern for all periods considered, V, or the slim part of F, will also reveal an erratic—irregularly zigzag type—pattern, but centered by and large around the Von Neumann path V^*. With prescribed consumption patterns that are more regular, more regular loci V and funnels are obtained. The most important general set of rules relevant here is as follows: In the S-case, with a prescribed consumption pattern which regularly involves a proportion of x over y higher (or lower) than the proportions of the Von Neumann path, most of the limiting path V—or of the slim part of the funnel—will proceed through x/y ratios higher (or lower) than that of V^*. The opposite rule applies for the Z-case.[26] Of course, with a consumption pattern replicating in its proportions the proportions of V^*, the path V with nonzero consumption still will tend to be asymptotic to V^*.

The rules just stated can be further refined and made more specific in some special cases: With prescribed unique consumption proportions different from those of V^* and a unique share of income consumed for all periods, there will be a ray passing through the origin V_c^*, different from the Von Neumann path V^*, playing the same role with respect to any actual paths or funnels as does the Von Neumann ray V^* with respect to any actual paths or funnels in the case of zero consumption. In particular, the turnpike theorem as stated in Chapter IX now applies to the case of nonzero consumption without alteration provided that it is stated with reference to V_c^* rather than with reference to V^*. The Von Neumann path V^* thus becomes, among paths corresponding to constant consumption proportions and a fixed share of income consumed, a special case where the fixed share is zero.

From the above general rules about the position of the V-path with respect to V^*, it logically follows that the new paths V_c^* will be above or below V^* (that is, what we now can describe as $V_{c=0}^*$) depending on the relation of the fixed proportions of consumption to the proportions of the "traditional" Von Neumann path V^*. In the S-case (Z-case) there will be a positive concordance (inverse

[26] Recall the definitions of the S-case and of the Z-case as situations involving productive processes relatively intensive in the input which is their output and relatively intensive in the input which is not their output.

relation) between the deviation of the consumption proportions from V^* and the deviation of V_c^* from V^*. It can be shown that what we have termed here "concordance" and "inverse relation" can actually be refined into "positive" and "negative" correlation. Indeed, the stronger the deviation of the prescribed consumption proportions from the proportions of V^*, the further, *ceteris paribus*, will be the "asymptote with consumption" V_c^* from V^*. A similar correlation exists between the prescribed share of income consumed—again *ceteris paribus*—and the degree of divergence between V^* and V_c^*.

But perhaps of greatest interest is the situation where consumption, with or without a fixed share of income consumed, is determined in each period through a process of maximization of utility with given relative prices (R) of the period. In that case—which includes the above situation of fixed-proportions consumption as a special case—there again will be a unique path $V \equiv F(\infty) \equiv f(-\infty)$ in whose immediate vicinity all long-range efficient paths will proceed for most of their duration (in the sense of the turnpike theorem). While not asymptotic to any ray through the origin—except in the special case of proportionality noted already—the path V will, as a general rule, reveal a smooth pattern whenever the income-consumption lines corresponding to the given utility function have a smooth form.

In concluding our general discussion, it may be useful to observe that the whole formulation of the problem of long-range growth can be altered when we allow nonzero consumption. Recall that in the traditional statement of the zero-consumption case the object is to determine the efficient path leading—after many periods—from a given initial endowment to a maximum level of capital stocks, the latter being in a prescribed proportion to each other (that is, the objective is to attain the furthest point along a ray through the origin). In our analysis we have introduced a small alteration, considering funnels of all possible paths, rather than individual paths, corresponding to a prescribed time horizon. But in both situations the objective is to maximize the terminal capital stocks.

By contrast, with positive levels of consumption permitted, the problem of long-range growth may be seen not so much in the maximization of terminal capital stocks, but rather—and in my opinion more realistically—in the preservation, over long periods, of maximal capital stocks as a "vehicle" or "carrier" of maximal levels of consumption. It is clear that in this context any intertemporally inefficient path is undesirable, because an efficient path could attain higher levels of consumption—with the same capital formation at least in some periods. But we know that all other paths besides $V \equiv F(\infty)$ must become inefficient sooner or later. And thus a society interested in a sustained optimal growth of capital and consumption in the long run should seek out the path V, common to all funnels. Any other path must lead to intertemporal inefficiency, or even to a complete impossibility of further production in a finite number of time periods. Of course, to the extent that we are in one of the special cases where a generalized Von Neumann ray V_c^* exists, and provided that terminal maximization is desired, a statement similar to the turnpike theorem can be made to the effect that "the society should seek a path within a small angle e of V_c^* for all but a limited number of periods, that number being independent of the total number of periods for which the long-range growth is envisioned, but depending on the size of e."

XIX. Proofs and other technical discussion underlying the case of nonzero consumption

As we suggested in the introduction to the preceding chapter, the analysis of long-range growth in a Von Neumann world can be presented under two distinct headings: convergence of the efficient funnels and of the loci f and f' toward a limiting locus V, and the actual position—or location—of V vis-à-vis the Von Neumann path or otherwise. This chapter is organized in such a manner. Because discussion under both headings, but especially under the first, is quite analogous to that presented in Chapters VIII and IX concerning the zero-consumption case, we will proceed quite rapidly here, assuming that the discussion of the two earlier chapters is familiar to the reader.

To further simplify and streamline our discussion we also assume throughout that x is relatively x-intensive and y is relatively y-intensive (that is, we will use the S-case) and that the production functions are of the smooth and linear-homogeneous variety, as assumed in the early chapters of the study. The reader may want to study situations involving the Z-case and/or fixed coefficients on his own, remembering that the transition between the no-consumption case and the consumption case is similar whether in the neoclassical situation or not. Moreover, we assume through the first part of our discussion—along with Dorfman, Samuelson, and Solow[27]—that nonzero levels of consumption, identical for each individual period and the same or different among periods, are exogenously given; the only proviso we make is that these levels are such that an efficient frontier T_i, giving levels of output after consumption available for production in the next period, is entirely outside a frontier T_{i+1}. Alternative assumptions of proportional consumptions in all periods, or that of prescribed indifference maps coupled with a prescribed level of income consumed, will be examined later.

With these introductory remarks in mind, let us now turn to Figure 17. T_i represents the efficient frontier attainable in period i from resources given by the frontier T_{i-1}, after prescribed consumption of $\bar{x}$ and $\bar{y}$ reflected by the vector cc' (or aa'). The locus T_i' is the locus of maximal attainable outputs—known to us from the zero-consumption case—starting from combinations of productive resources given by T_{i-1}. In a similar manner, any other T-locus is derived from a corresponding T'-locus by substracting the prescribed consumption levels of each period.

As indicated by the constructions involving points a, a', g, c, c', and d, the loci $f(-1)$ and $f'(-1)$ are—as they were in the zero-consumption case—loci of points on all efficient funnels $F(n+1)$ one period before the

[27] Dorfman, Samuelson, and Solow, *op. cit.*, chap. 12.

target (or terminal) period $n + 1$; in other words, $f(-1)$ and $f'(-1)$ are loci of intersection between the T_n's and the $F(n + 1)$'s for $n = 1, 2, 3, \ldots$. One such point d is obtained at the point of tangency between T_{i-1} and an isoquant (not in Figure 17) belonging to a homogeneous Scitovsky map defined (in the sense explained in Chapter VIII and corresponding to Conclusion IV of Chapter VII) by the prescribed $\bar{x}$- and $\bar{y}$-production functions and output proportions of point c'. It will be noted that except for the vector cc' this construction is quite analogous to that in the zero-consumption case; note that in that case $f(-1)$ would have had to pass through d', the point of tangency between T_{i-1} and an isoquant of product y

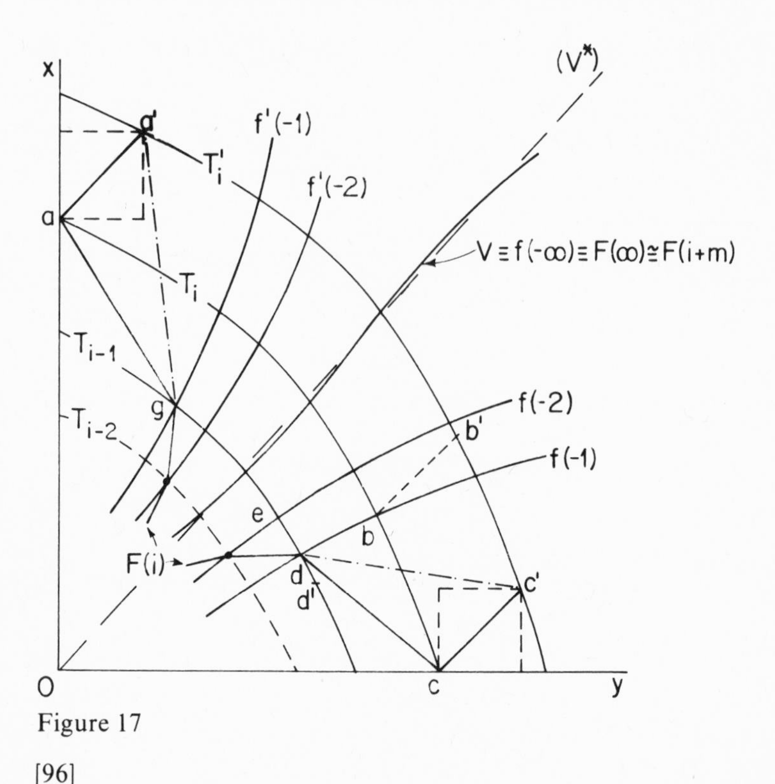

Figure 17

(the isoquant is not in Figure 17). By virtue of Conclusion IV of Chapter VII, d' must be below d on T_{i-1}, because d' generates a gross output of $\bar{y}$ only, while d generates intertemporally efficient outputs of both $\bar{x}$ and $\bar{y}$, and $\bar{x}$ is relatively x-intensive. All points of $f(-1)$ are obtained, from all points such as c, that is, from the intercepts between the y-axis and the T-loci. The locus $f(-2)$ —and analogously for $f'(-2)$—is then obtained from all points of $f(-1)$, such as d and b. For example, e is a point of tangency between T_{i-1} and a Scitovsky isoquant given by the underlying technologies and product proportions of b', linked to b through the constant consumption vector $\mathbf{bb'}$ ($\mathbf{cc'}$). By virtue of Conclusion IV of Chapter VII, $f(-2)$ must be above $f(-1)$—and $f'(-2)$ below $f'(-1)$—and similarly for higher index loci f and f'. The loci $f(-3)$ and $f'(-3)$ are enclosed by $f(-2)$ and $f'(-2)$, the $f(-4)$ loci by the $f(-3)$ loci, and so forth, ad infinitum, until the locus $V \equiv f(-\infty) \equiv F(\infty)$ is reached. Actually, the locus V in Figure 17 can be thought of as representing approximately, in the vicinity of T_i, all funnels $F(i + m)$, for m larger than, say, twenty. This is so because of the rapid convergence of the f loci—actually more rapid than in the zero-consumption case (note that d is northwest of d' in the diagram)—toward V.

It is thus clear that on the assumptions made—in particular, the prescribed levels of nonzero consumption for each period—the funnels $F(n)$ of efficient paths terminating in period n will tend to become arbitrarily "slim" at a given T_i for n sufficiently large. That the same must hold with various alternative specifications regarding the consumption levels should be clear. For example, suppose that it is postulated that a prescribed level of income is to be spent on consumption in each period, and an ordinal utility index corresponding to a prescribed utility function (identical or different for each period) is to be maximized. Since the introduction of nonzero consumption levels does not change anything about the variation of relative prices R and $\bar{R}$ along efficient paths, as established in Chapter IV, the efficient frontiers T_n and T'_n will again tend toward linearity and relative prices $R_n = \bar{R}_n$ toward R^*.[28] Actually, except for situations involving extremely divergent factor proportions in $\bar{x}$ and $\bar{y}$—as we have pointed out already in Chapter X—this convergence, geometric in nature, should be very rapid. But with a constant share of income consumed and relative prices just about constant and equal to the slope of T'—as the reader will verify through a conventional diagram—the consumption vector in each period will be just about constant also (as it was in the previously studied case with vectors **aa**$'$, **bb**$'$, or **cc**$'$). And thus, at least for n large enough to have the desired effects of linearization on T'_n, the same as above holds: the loci f and f' will converge towards V.

Having argued the convergence of the funnels and loci f towards V, we can now study the position of V itself. In our more careful exposition we will limit ourselves to the case of constant proportion of income consumed and constant consumption-proportions for all periods. As we have pointed out in the preceding chapter, this case yields some very regular and well-behaved results, generalizations of the Von Neumann path and of the turnpike theorem. These "careful" results we will then use to indi-

[28] Recall the distinction between T and T' introduced earlier in this chapter and illustrated in Figure 17: The former symbol pertains to the efficient post-consumption resource combinations while the latter represents growth outputs before consumption of a particular period.

cate, in a more approximate manner, some rules of behavior for the path $V \equiv F(\infty) \equiv f(-\infty)$ in more general and irregular situations where a Von Neumann-type linear asymptote does not exist.

In what follows we rely a good deal on the analysis of Chapter V; the reader thus may find it useful to reread it at this stage. Figure 18, except for the fact that we now consider a situation of nonzero consumption, contains the same elements as Figure 4. The slopes of AA, BB, and DD in Figure 18 reflect the Von Neumann relative-price ratio (as obtained in Chapter IV), $R^* = \bar{R}^*$. In the neoclassical situation considered here, the intertem-

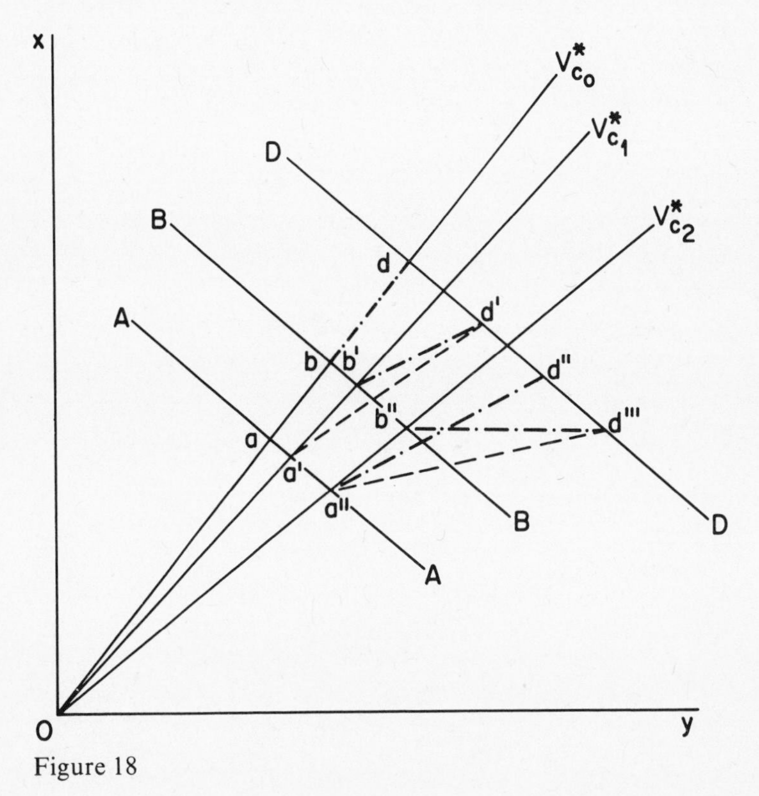

Figure 18

porally efficient output derivable from inputs indicated by point a, with relative prices $R^* = \bar{R}^*$ (the marginal rates of transformation and substitution at a), is given by point d. We know from Chapter IV that at d the marginal rates again must equal $R^* = \bar{R}^*$; this, plus the fact that d is on the same ray through the origin with a, guarantees that $0ad$ is V^*, the traditional Von Neumann path with zero consumption.

Suppose now that it so happens that consumption of $\bar{x}$ and $\bar{y}$, in proportions identical to those of V^*, is to take place in each period, with the only further stipulation that the proportion of income consumed (the income is measured here by the segment ad) not be larger than one. In that case the economy again will progress from point a, indefinitely, along V^*—the ray marked in the diagram as $V^*_{c_0}$. The only difference from the previous situation is that with nonzero consumption the resources available for the production in the second period will be at b (rather than at d), assuming that the segment bd represents the prescribed level of consumption. It is also obvious that the case where, with the same consumption proportions, the average propensity to consume is to remain indefinitely at the level $C = (bd)/(ad)$ is only a special case of the situation with variable C; $V^*_{c_0}$ again must be the relevant growth path.

Consider now the situation which is identical to that with a constant C just discussed except that the consumption proportions now are to be those given by the slope of $b'd'$. It is clear that starting from a, as before, the output of the economy would again be found at d and relative prices still would be $R^* = \bar{R}^*$, but the resources available for production in the second period would be on BB, northwest of b. Given the data implicit in the construction—as the reader will easily verify—such an endowment point would within three or four periods lead the efficient path (from a) to a situation involving production of only $\bar{x}$ and thus termination of intertemporally efficient growth. It is thus necessary to correct, so to speak, the distortion imputable to the fact that the new consumption proportions are biased relative to those of $V^*_{c_0}$, by shifting point a along AA to the position a'—of course, retaining the stable Von Neumann price ratio $R^* = \bar{R}^*$. This correction yields a production point d', which is intertemporally efficient, and a corresponding postconsumption point b'. $R^* = \bar{R}^*$ being the relative prices at both a' and b', and the two points being on a ray through the origin $V^*_{c_1}$, it is clear that $V^*_{c_1}$ is an equilibrium growth path (corresponding, of course, to a and R^*) provided that the share of income consumed remains at the level $(bd)/(ad)$. Note that a ray through 0 and d' (not in the diagram) would be the corresponding locus of all preconsumption points of production, the rate of progress along that path being the same as along $V^*_{c_0}$, that is, $r = (a'b')/(0a')$.

A similar construction describing an economy consuming product $\bar{y}$ only leads to an even more extreme position of the equilibrium growth path, namely $V^*_{c_2}$. It is clear that for consumption patterns biased toward x (relative to $V^*_{c_0}$) the equilibrium growth path will be found above $V^*_{c_0}$.[29] It is also apparent from the construction involving a'' and d'', where the average savings are zero and the consumption proportions the same as those underlying $V^*_{c_1}$, that an increase in the share of income consumed,

[29] It should also be clear to the reader by now that the opposite relations between $V^*_{c_0}$ and the other equilibrium paths will prevail in the Z-case.

ceteris paribus, will increase the divergence between the traditional Von Neumann path $V^*_{c_0}$ and the equilibrium path. Of course, if the consumption proportions are those of $V^*_{c_0}$ then, as we have seen above, no divergence is possible.

The rays such as $V^*_{c_1}$ or $V^*_{c_2}$ play the same role with regard to efficient funnels and growth paths with constant consumption rates and proportions as did V^* in the zero-consumption case. The reasoning behind this conjecture is the same as that which leads us to the turnpike theorem. An efficient funnel $F(n)$ corresponding to a distant time horizon n and to $\bar{y}$-biased consumption proportions is illustrated in Figure 19. Most of the slim part of the funnel proceeds in the immediate vicinity of the $V^*_{c_1}$. This is so because, as we have seen, any funnel must contain V, and V is an efficient path asymptotic to $V^*_{c_1}$.

As before, the turnpike theorem again must hold. Suppose that n is large, and, say, ten more periods are added. We now would have a new funnel $F(n + 10)$, entirely contained by $F(n)$ in Figure 19 in the region below T_n. Recalling that, with n large, T_n again must be infinitesimally near linearity (the reader should not be misled by the drawing, where the concavity of T_n was made quite conspicuous) with a slope infinitesimally near $R^* = \bar{R}^*$, we find that the loci f and f' in the region above T_n will be infinitesimally near being rays through the origin. But if this is so, the addition of ten periods to the time horizon cannot augment—by definition of the loci f and f'—the number of periods when the funnel (that is, all efficient paths corresponding to the time horizon of the funnel) is further away from $V^*_{c_1}$ than a stipulated small angle e.

Suppose now that, with the same T_1, a growth situation is envisaged where the same share of income as in the preceding situation is expended on consumption every year. The consumption proportions also are y-biased, as before, but y, in addition, has a greater than unitary income elasticity, while x has a less than unitary income elasticity. With increasing income, as time goes on, the y-bias will now be becoming stronger and stronger. We have shown above that the corresponding funnels $F(n)$ will be converging toward V with increasing n; but what will be the position of V? It is intuitively obvious—and the reader may want to transform the intuition into a rigor-

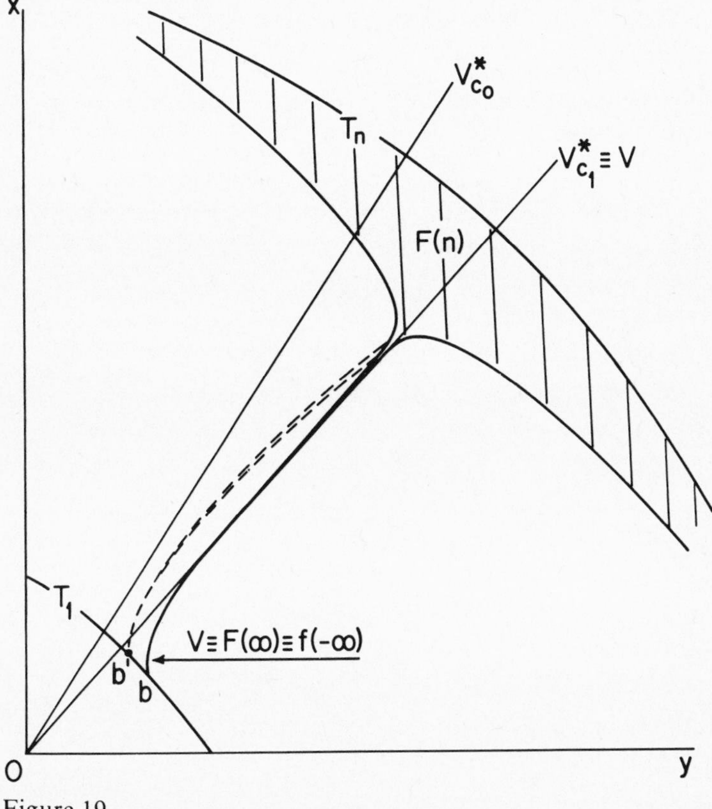

Figure 19

ous proof—that V again will be y-biased with regard to $V^*_{c_0}$ and that as the consumption-proportion bias strengthens over time (with increasing real income), so will that of V. Such a pattern is indicated in Figure 19 by means of the broken-line alteration of the funnel $F(n)$.

XX. Production functions with fixed coefficients: joint production

We now face an important and not entirely easy task: to abandon the assumption of single-product technologies and transplant, so to speak, the analysis into the more traditional and more conventional framework of joint-product activities. As far as the assumptions are concerned, we will thus parallel to a large extent a recent work by Professor Koopmans, "Economic Growth at a Maximal Rate."[30] From the point of view of methodology and exposition, however, we will follow as closely as possible what has been done in the preceding nineteen chapters, and present the present material as a generalization of the foregoing analysis. We will treat only the *S*-case.[31] The reader again is invited to study the *Z*-case on his own. Moreover, we adhere in what follows to the conventional assumptions of zero consumption and no technological change. We also retain in the first part of

[30] *Op. cit.*

[31] It should be noted that with joint products a new definition, including the traditional one, must be adopted: The *S*-case is one where the same relative intensity is found between two activities on the side of inputs and outputs.

this chapter the assumption of only two industries (activities). Our purpose, let it be recalled, is to study the Von Neumann maximal growth path and other intertemporally efficient paths, together with what we may term the "turnpike properties" of such paths.

Because we want to present our analysis as a generalization of the single-product case, it will be most expedient to restate some of our preceding analysis in a streamlined manner that will lend itself well to the desired generalizations. Recall the case of fixed coefficients and single-product activities studied in Chapters XV, XVI, and XVII; it may also be useful to the reader at this point to recall Chapter IV. Now consider Figure 20; it contains nothing but what is known to us already. Together with the origin 0 and the coordinate axes x and y, points a_0,

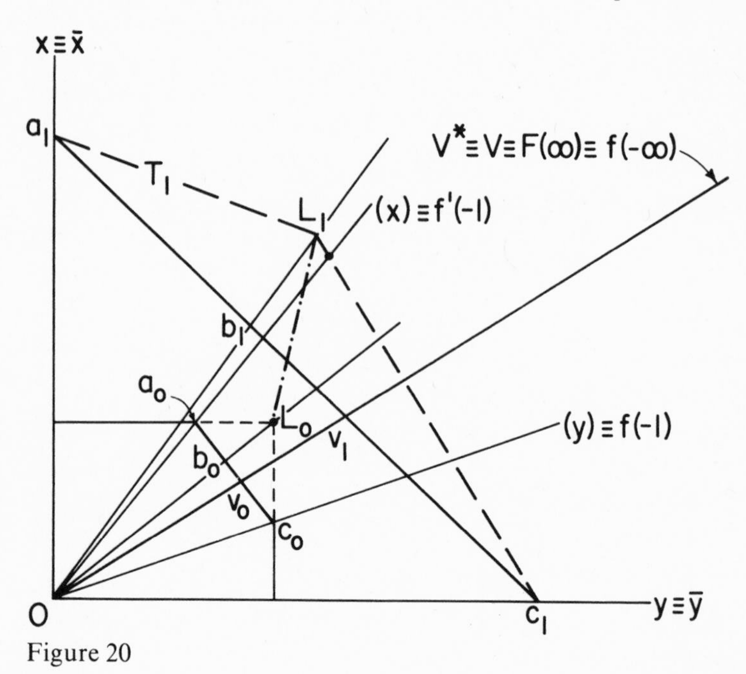

Figure 20

c_0, a_1, and c_1 completely specify a growth situation. Note that inputs in industry x at a_0 lead to output at a_1, and similarly for c_0 and c_1 with respect to the y-industry; moreover, a_0 and c_0 exhaust entirely the initial supplies of x and y, as given by L_0, respectively. As we know from our discussion in Chapter XV, the technologies and initial endowments as specified lead to T_1, shown in the diagram, T_1 analogously leads to T_2, and so forth.

All this can be expressed in a different manner. The triangle $a_0c_0L_0$ is *transformed* into the triangle $a_1c_1L_1$ through a transformation defined by the two given production functions of x and y. It may be useful to visualize the transformation in a mechanistic way. Suppose we have a simple machine whose one arm is attached to a pencil, and with that pencil we trace the triangle $a_0c_0L_0$; the machine then has another handle (or arm) with another pencil, and the latter traces the locus of corresponding full-employment outputs based on the two given technologies and the inputs corresponding to the position of the point of the first pencil. What the second arm of the machine traces, as we know already, is the triangle $a_1c_1L_1$, whose outer frontier, represented by the broken line, is nothing but T_1.

There are some simple rules of conduct which the machine must follow whether or not we are in the single-product situation. They are so simple that we can state them without proof, leaving the verification to the reader's labors or, for that matter, to his intuition. The first is that a movement of the first pencil along a straight line must correspond to a straight movement of the second pencil; the second, closely related, is that an inch of movement of the first pencil along a given line must correspond to a constant distance traveled by the second pencil. The third rule is that a movement along a ray through the origin by the first pencil corresponds to a movement by the second pencil, also along a ray through the origin. As a fourth rule it can easily be shown that parallel straight movements of the first pencil lead to parallel straight movements of the second pencil. The fifth and last rule is that a clockwise rotation of a line traced by the first pencil corresponds to a clockwise rotation of the line traced by the second pencil and vice versa.[32]

We can now put our machine to work, placing the first pencil at a_0; by definition, the machine places the second pencil at a_1. Now we start tracing the line a_0c_0, while the machine traces a_1c_1. Two important points are encountered by the first pencil. The first is b_0, reached after about $2/5$ of the entire distance has been traveled, where the first pencil encounters the ray $0L_0$—at that stage the second pencil is at b_1, which by our second rule is also about $2/5$ of the distance between a_1 and c_1. From b_0 we can take a side-excursion along a ray through the origin, all the way to L_0; by the second and third rules the second pencil finds the very important (Leontief) point L_1, on the ray $0b_1$, about $1/3$ of the distance $0b_1$ beyond b_1 (observe that L_0 is about $1/3$ of the distance $0b_0$ beyond b_0).

Returning from the excursion, we continue with the first pencil from b_0 toward c_0. We encounter the second important landmark at v_0—it is at this point that an observer placed at 0 sees the points of both pencils coincide, the second pencil having reached v_1. At this stage, defining the Von Neuman path V^*, the second pencil in its "radial" chase of the first pencil overtakes that pencil, never to be caught up with again along the stretch ac.

[32] Of course we have to recall here our assumption of the S-case.

The rest of the itinerary to c_0 is uneventful; and so, in fact, is all the remaining part of the round trip leading the first pencil from c_0 to L_0 and from L_0 back to a_0. Since L_1 and V^* were established already, our first rule assures us that all of T_1 is now known.

With all that has been said thus far in mind, we can turn to the situations involving joint-product activities. Retaining the assumption of two activities (with two products we know that a larger number never is necessary), we will proceed by discussing three distinct situations. These three cases are almost exhaustive of the possibilities at hand; the minor gaps that remain we will cover less rigorously at the end of the chapter.

The first two major cases we want to discuss can be termed "well behaved" in the sense that their Von Neumann paths are based on both activities and, hence, involve full employment of both resources at all times. The first of the two is one where both activities can produce $\bar{x}$ and $\bar{y}$, but the x-input-intensive activity (still referred to as the x-activity) has outputs even more x-intensive, and the y-input-intensive activity has outputs which are even more y-intensive. This situation, again defined fully by points a_0, c_0, a_1, and c_1, is illustrated in Figure 21. Its important characteristic, similar to that encountered for the no-joint-product case, is that the range of output lines $(\bar{x})$ and $(\bar{y})$ entirely contains the input range (x)-(y). From this it follows that if we use our machine (into which were fed the new joint-product data) and if we travel with the first pencil from a_0 to c_0, the second pencil traveling from a_1 to c_1 must catch up with the first pencil, the latter (first pencil) being somewhere between a_0—this happens when the two pencils are at v_1 and v_0 respectively—and c_0; hence there is a proportional growth path based on both activities. Since that path is also indefinitely efficient, it is V^*, a Von Neumann path. Actually, the situation distinctly resembles the one with single outputs, except that the output rays $(\bar{x})$ and $(\bar{y})$ now form an angle of less than 90 degrees. The rays (x) and (y) again are nothing but the loci $f'(-1)$ and $f(-1)$ of points on efficient funnels one period prior to termination; termination now again takes place at $(\bar{x})$ and $(\bar{y})$, marked $f(0)$ and $f'(0)$ respectively in Figure 21. Using our machine, it is possible to trace $f(-2)$ and $f'(-2)$ by the first pencil in such a way as to keep the second pencil on $f(-1)$ and $f'(-1)$. Because the latter two loci are rays through the

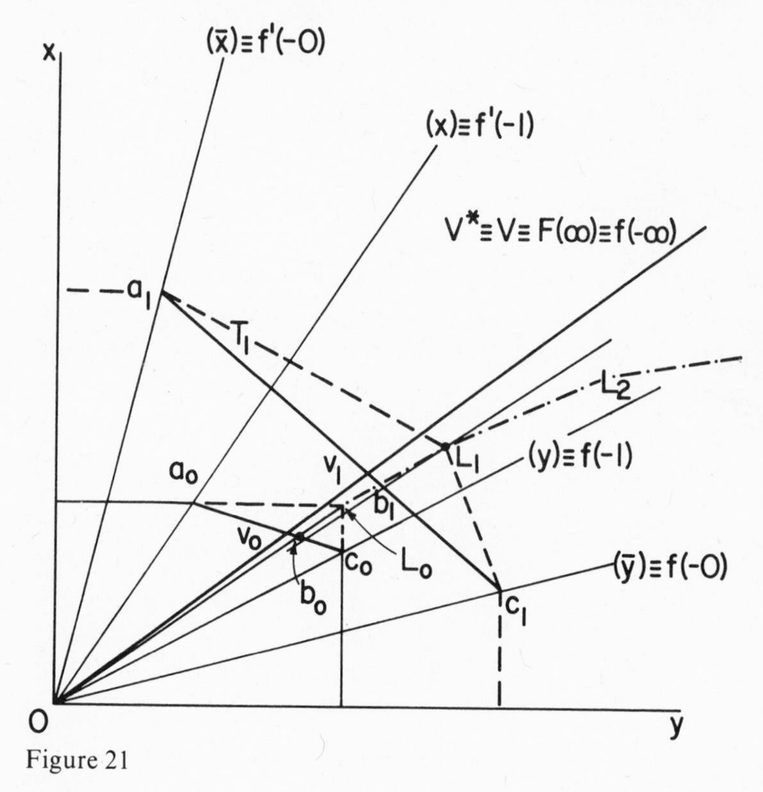

Figure 21

origin, so will be the two loci traced by the first pencil. In a similar manner the $f(-3)$ loci are traced, and so forth; the limit of the process is again reached at $V^* \equiv V \equiv f(-\infty) \equiv F(\infty)$. Thus all long-range growth paths originate at, or in the immediate vicinity of, the intersection between T_1 and V^*.

The convergence of the loci f towards V^* should be obvious from the way a_1c_1 was constructed through our machine from a_0c_0. Recall that when the first pencil is at a_0, the second is at a_1; then move the first along a_1c_1 so as to have the second on (x) in the diagram. This defines a further point on a_0c_0 which is on, and defines, $f(-2)$. Thus the process is continued; it clearly cannot transgress V^* because if it ever reached V^* (we know that this happens after an infinite number of steps) the point marked off on a_0c_0 would correspond to a point also on V^* and no further movement could take place along a_0c_0 in the southeast direction.

Of course, recalling that the f-loci actually are loci of tangency (contact) between the T-frontiers and fixed-coefficient isoquants of the Scitovsky variety, some might object that we also have to know that in the relevant ranges all the T-loci actually are negatively sloped. The objection is valid, but in the situation here discussed the slopes of all T's effectively are negative. Without going into the complete proof of the matter, let it only be noted that the first transformation locus T_1 fulfills the condition of a negative slope and that by our fifth rule of this chapter the segment of T_i and L_i must be getting steeper and that below L_i flatter with increasing $i = 2, 3, 4, \ldots$, the two having a common (necessarily negative) slope for $i = \infty$. The same may not hold in other situations involving joint production, however; our second "well behaved" case—to which we will turn presently—is an important illustration.

But before we turn to the next case a few words regarding the turnpike theorem are in order. Although the rays $(\bar{x})$ and $(\bar{y})$ have now moved away from the coordinate axes, everything that has been said or proved about the turnpike properties of efficient paths in the single-output case also holds in the joint-product case thus far discussed. The linearity of the loci f and f' together with their convergence towards V^* is all that is needed as a proof of the turnpike theorem in its generalized version, analogous to that presented for the Leontief case in Chapter XVII.

Let us now turn briefly to the next case; it is illustrated in Figure 22 and is just the reverse of the preceding one. The input range (x)-(y) is now wider than, and entirely

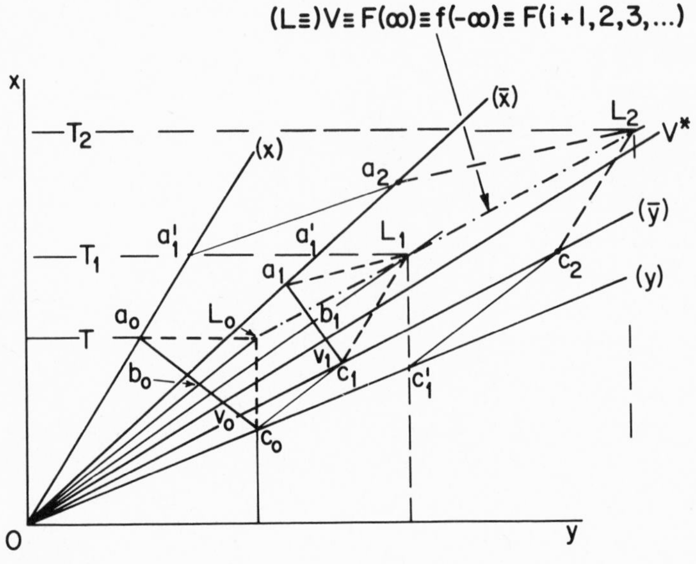

Figure 22

contains, the output range $(\bar{x})$-$(\bar{y})$. Using our machine in very much the same way as we did in the preceding case, we transform the initial triangle $a_0c_0L_0$—defined by the initial endowments and the technologies—into the triangle $a_1c_1L_1$. While doing this we again identify points v_0 and v_1 and thus define V^*. Obviously, the only efficient point on the transformation is L_1, and T_1 thus becomes the rectangle defined by L_1. By our fourth rule we know that the second-period triangle $a_2c_2L_2$, obtained through our machine from the triangle $a_1'c_1'L_1$, must have its own positively sloped sides parallel to the corresponding sides of the first-period triangle $a_1c_1L_1$. The important fact is, however, that the angular distance of L_1 from V^* is less than the angular distance of L_0 from V^*, that the angular distance of L_2 from V^* is less than the angular distance of L_1 from V^*, and so forth. For L_0 and L_1 (and analogously for L_1 and L_2) this is a result of the fact that as the first pencil of the machine moves from a_0 toward c_0 and reaches b_0, it could not have caught up yet (angularly) with the second pencil. This is so by virtue of the second rule and because the same angular position is reached only at V^*.

The third and further generations of triangles acL are all derived in an analogous fashion, and the argument just used for $i = 0, 1, 2$ to show the convergence of the angular distances between L_i and V^* holds for all i, indefinitely. In other words, the only efficient path L_0, $L_1, L_2, \ldots$ is asymptotic to V^* and hence is also the path V. But as such it is also $F(\infty)$ and $f(-\infty)$. Moreover, since any efficient path directed toward T_n must proceed along V for all but the last period (in which the appropriate x-y mix is reached by disposal), the path V at any L_i also represents all efficient funnels $F(i + 1, 2, \ldots, \infty)$.

The turnpike theorem now presents itself in its degenerate form: With F identical to V for all but the last period and V asymptotic to V^*, it is clear that (1) F can be within e, arbitrarily small, of V^* for any fraction of the total time span provided that the time span is made long enough, and (2) extension of the time span cannot add any periods when F is further from V^* (measured in degrees) than e.

Before turning to the remaining cases, let it be noted that in the two situations just discussed, and termed "well behaved," it is immaterial whether the initial endowment point L_0 is one permitting of full employment of resources in the first period (as it did in our two illustrations) or not (that is, whether L_0 falls within the input range (x)-(y) or not). The relevant characteristics of the two cases, besides those regarding the ranges of the inputs (x)-(y) and outputs $(\bar{x})$-$(\bar{y})$, are: always negative slopes of lines such as $a_i L_i$ and $L_i c_i$ (whether both or only one is applicable) for the first well-behaved situation, and positive slopes of such lines in the second well-behaved situation, for any and all initial endowments.

The remaining cases are—in at least two distinct respects—combinations of elements taken from the two "well-behaved" situations just studied. The first important characteristic is an overlapping or a complete difference of the input range (x)-(y) and the output range $(\bar{x})$-$(\bar{y})$—the latter is illustrated in Figure 23. As the reader will easily verify, (using our transformation machine if he so desires), no proportional efficient growth path V^* involving both activities and full employment (as it was in the two well behaved cases) is now possible. Use of a single activity and less than full employment of one of the two productive resources will now generally

be the outcome for most or all of the duration of an efficient path. The Von Neumann path will then be the output ray of the activity actually used, and of course it will generally not involve full employment of resources. All efficient funnels will coincide with V for all but the last period and with V^*, in the long run, for all but the last and possibly a few early periods (immediately following period 0). To find the Von Neumann path knowing that only one activity will be used, of course, the easiest method is to try out each activity and see what is intertemporally more efficient. As the reader can easily verify,

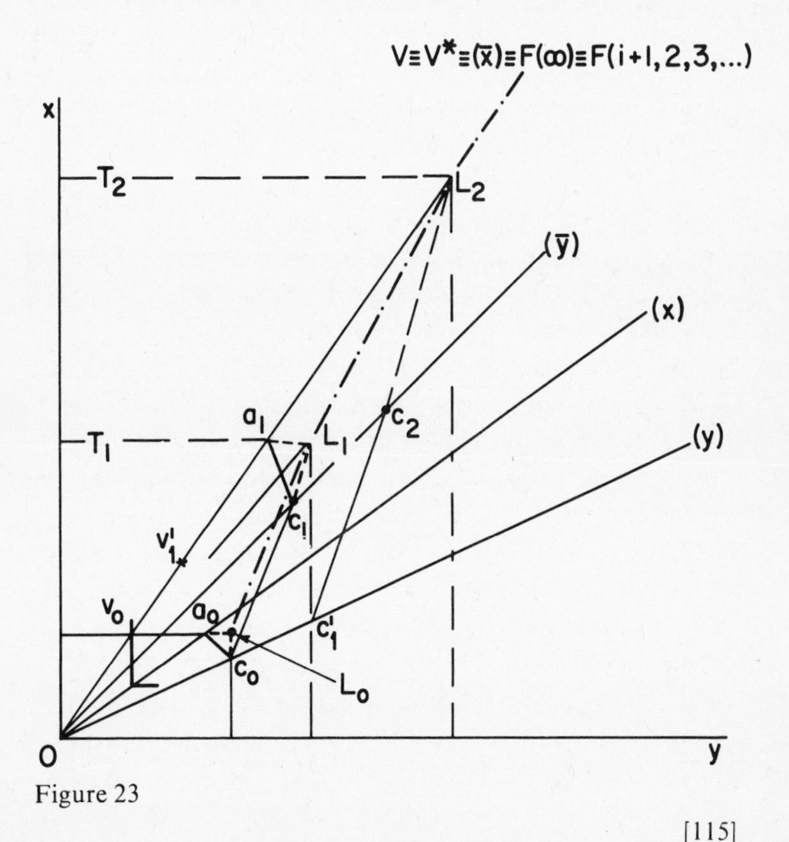

Figure 23

the turnpike theorem again is trivial, and so is its proof, when only one joint-product activity is involved in the Von Neumann path.

Another combination of our two well-behaved cases arises when the transformation of the initial segments a_0L_0 and L_0c_0 leads to segments a_1L_1 and L_1c_1 having slopes of different sign. Actually, this can happen whether the input and output ranges overlap or not. In either case, the difference of signs of the transformed segments in the first period predicts an unavoidable elimination of one of the two activities from any efficient growth path at a later stage, and thus it indicates existence of a one-activity Von Neumann path. Actually, as the reader may want to verify, the activity which must disappear and hence which cannot be included in V^* is the one whose output ray—such as $(\bar{x})$ or $(\bar{y})$ in our diagrams—is adjacent to the positively sloped segments.

Most of these conclusions are illustrated in Figure 23. An initial triangle $a_0c_0L_0$ is transformed here into the triangle $a_1c_1L_1$ by means of our transformation machine containing the technological information reflected by points a_0, a_1, c_0, and c_1. The input and output ranges here are entirely different and thus no full-employment two-activity proportional growth path is possible. Moreover, c_1L_1 now has a positive slope and a_1L_1 a negative slope, and thus, as enunciated above and as the construction indicates, activity y disappears—it does so already in the second period as shown by point L_2. The ray $(\bar{x})$ thus is the Von Neumann ray, and it coincides with V and all the efficient funnels after L_2. The turnpike theorem is again trivial and obvious. The rate of expansion along V^* is indicated by points v_0 and v_1'. Note that the outputs at v_1' correspond to the L-shaped isoquant passing through v_0, and that v_1' is obtained from the corner of that isoquant by means of a line parallel to $a_0 a_1$.

In concluding this chapter we can summarize all our findings regarding the turnpike theorem, integrating the single-product and the joint-product cases into one general situation. Of course, we retain for the moment the assumption that there are only two activities in existence—and also the assumptions of fixed coefficients, of two products, and of the S-case made at the outset of the present chapter (recall that the Z-case generally leads to analogous results). First, it can be concluded that the "pure" catenary turnpike profile—resembling a rope attached at the two extremities of an efficient path and attracted in a gravity-like manner toward the Von Neumann path V^*—really never arises with fixed coefficients (it is actually encountered only for the smooth neoclassical situation). We encounter the pattern just described, however, only slightly modified, in the single-product situation and the joint-product situation dealt with first in this chapter (both slopes of $a_1 L_1$ and $L_1 c_1$ negative and the output range entirely covering the input range)—the modification being that all efficient paths come nearest to V^* in the first period and diverge from that ray thereafter. The remaining two situations—that corresponding to both actual or potential[33] $a_1 L_1$ and $L_1 c_1$ positively sloped and that where the two segments have different slopes—we have termed trivial because the proofs of the corresponding turnpike theorems are obvious. In both

[33]Note that for some initial endowments only one of the two segments may exist in period one (at T_I); in such a situation it should be tested what slope the other segment would have if appropriate initial endowments were available.

instances all efficient funnels proceed along, and coincide with, V except for the terminal period, when—so to speak—the funnels open up in a fanlike manner to attain the whole 90-degree span of the terminal efficient frontier T_i. Since, moreover, V is asymptotic to V^*—reaching V^* after an infinite number of steps in the first trivial case (the second well-behaved case) and after a finite number of steps in the second—it is clear that an efficient funnel $F(n)$ can be made to fall within an arbitrarily small angle e of V^* for any prescribed fraction of the total number of periods n, provided that we pick an n large enough; recalling that each funnel "opens up" only in the last (nth) period, it is equally clear that the *absolute* number of periods when $F(n + h)$ is further than e from V^* cannot exceed the number of periods when $F(n)$ is further than e from V^*.

We may now turn briefly to the more general case where the society has a choice between, not two, but a large number of activities capable of transforming inputs of x and y in one period into outputs of the same two products in the next period. Obviously, each particular growth solution will depend on the specific data defining the case, and there are so many possibilities that an exhaustive analysis of the type just presented for two activities is inconceivable. However, some general remarks, not necessarily proved in full, can be made on the subject.

The first, intuitively obvious, is that whatever the number of activities—indeed, the neoclassical case studied earlier is nothing but a case of an infinite number of activities—prescribed initial conditions and a prescribed set of potential activities lead to (or define) a set of efficient transformation loci T_i similar to those known to us from the rest of our analysis. As before, these loci must all be concave; note for example that with two triangles such as $a_1 L_1 c_1$ (in any of the diagrams of this chapter) which are now possible with more than two activities, a convexity would seem to appear in the region between the two vertexes L_1—but this is impossible because the line connecting the two vertexes L_1 itself is a feasible locus, obtainable (with full employment) as a linear combination of the two two-activity "joint" activities underlying the two triangles.

If an efficient path goes through a region such as that just described between the two vertexes L_1, that path will clearly be based on more than two activities. For long-range paths, however, this is generally possible only in the early and the very late stages of the growth process (that is, at T_i's with low i's and i's just short of the terminal period). The intermediate stages of every efficient path will be based on only two activities, activities underlying the Von Neumann ray V^*, and will be located in the immediate vicinity of V^*. The Von Neumann path itself is determined by considering all conceivable pairs of activities (with n activities there will be $n(n-1)/2$ such pairs) in the way shown earlier in this chapter for a single pair of activities, and picking the ray corresponding to the highest proportional growth rate r^*.

Since we do not want to use mathematics in the present study, it is not easy to prove the proposition that with two products V^* will never need more than two activities. However, a verbal sketch of the underlying reasoning may be useful. Suppose that we have found V^* in the way just pointed out and have identified the corresponding optimal pair of activities. A third activity now is selected, and a prescribed very small dose thereof is introduced, together with the two optimal activities, the requirement again being to find a maximal proportional path. One such path will be found—generally involving a new set of input and output proportions—with a new proportional growth rate r_0. Now it must be clear that r_0 cannot exceed r^*. This is so because had the introduction of a small dose of the third activity increased r, then —because we are in a completely linear world—it would have paid to keep introducing further doses of the third activity, thereby further increasing r, until one of the original two activities was eliminated; and this would have left us again with two activities and r higher than r^*, which is a contradiction.

Index

INDEX